Americ

THE QUEST

Sandra Widener

Globe Fearon Educational Publisher
A Division of Simon & Schuster
Upper Saddle River, New Jersey

Project Editors: Keisha N. Carter, Lynn Kloss, Ann Clarkson
Poetry Writer and Editor: J. N. Fox
Director of Editorial and Marketing: Diane Galen
Executive Editor: Joan Carrafiello
Production Director: Kurt Scherwatzky
Production Editor: Alan Dalgleish
Marketing Manager: Margaret Rakus
Assistant Marketing Manager: Donna Frasco
Interior Electronic Design: Mimi Raihl
Art Direction: Armando Baez
Illustrator: Jose Miralles
Electronic Page Production: Mimi Raihl/Elaine Kilcullen
Cover Design: Sheree Goodman Design
Cover Photo: Photo Credit/© Jose Carrillo

Photos: p. 44 UPI/Bettmann; **p. 67** © Phil Cantor
Poetry: p.26 Bobbi Katz for *"My Basketball"*, Copyright © 1996 by Bobbi Katz; **p. 77** *A Call of Everest* reprinted by permission of author

Printed in the United States of America.
2 3 4 5 6 7 8 9 10 00 99 98

ISBN:0-8359-3355-5

GLOBE FEARON EDUCATIONAL PUBLISHER
A Division of Simon & Schuster
Upper Saddle River, New Jersey

Contents

To the Student

You are about to begin an adventure. Between the covers of this book are men hunting for gold. There is a famous dancer who was told she was too tall to be a star. There is love. There is courage. There is danger.

All the works focus on one theme: The Quest. The people in this book are looking for something. This something may be fame. It may be a world record in sports. Sometimes these people will do anything to reach their dreams. You may find that you, too, want them to reach their goals.

Within this book are many different kinds of writing. There are short stories and profiles of people. There are interviews and newspaper articles. There are poems. All of these selections show the many ways that people express themselves.

When you read these works, notice how the writing differs. A newspaper article reports what happened. A letter tells how a person is feeling. An interview shows you someone's point of view. A play helps you understand how different people feel.

Above all, we hope you enjoy this book. Some of the people in these stories may have problems like yours. Some stories may help you think about what other people face in their lives. In one selection, you might imagine you are a member of a rock band trying for a big break. In another, think about whether you would risk your life to find a cure for a disease. Step into other people's shoes. Settle into this book and let your mind soar.

Before You Read

Dan Jansen was the best speed skater in the world. Could he get over the tragedy in his life and prove it in the Olympics?

Dan Jansen: From Heartbreak to Victory

The 1988 Olympics in Canada should have been a wonderful time for Dan Jansen. He was one of the best speed skaters the world had ever seen. On ice, he seemed to enter a different world. His strong, smooth strides sent him around the course with ease. People watched him skate with wonder. He made it look easy.

But Dan Jansen left for the Calgary Olympics in 1988 with a lot on his mind. His much-loved sister Jane was dying of cancer. The decision to go had been hard to make. What if she died while he was there? Jane was sure what he should do. "Go," she told him. "You have to go."

Jane's encouragement didn't help on February 14, 1988. It was the day Dan Jansen was to race in the 500-meter speed skating event. At six that morning, Dan got a call from home. "We want you to say good-bye to Jane," his mother said. "She won't be able to answer, but she will be able to understand you." Jane was not expected to live through the day.

Dan got on the phone. He told Jane he loved her. "I'm going to win that race tonight for you," he said. Then his mother got back on the phone. Dan asked her if he should skate.

"You know Jane would want you to, Dan," she told him.

Dan Jansen, the best hope for the United States to

win a gold medal in skating, was in tears. Four hours later, Jane died.

The U.S. skating team met. They all decided to dedicate their races that day to Jane. Dan was having his own doubts. *Jane is dead. Should I be here?*

"The eyes of the world are on Dan Jansen," said the ABC reporter. Everyone knew about Jane's death. Everyone was watching to see what he would do.

That night, Dan Jansen skated. "I wasn't the same as usual," he wrote in his diary that night. The starter gun went off. Dan was off. But as he went around a turn, he slipped and fell. He spun into another skater. Around the world, you could hear the disappointment. It was the one race Dan had wanted to win. Instead, he was down and out of the race. It was a bitter time. To lose—on top of his sister's death?

There was one more chance. Dan skated four days later. It was the 1,000-meter race. Once again, he said he was skating for Jane. He took off like a rocket, leading the field. And then—he hit the ice. Dan had caught the edge of a skate. He was down.

Why would one of the best skaters the world has known fall twice during the Olympics? Dan Jansen wrote later, "I knew I just could not bring myself to win. It wasn't right, it wasn't just, that I should win a medal when my sister was not yet buried."

Dan Jansen continued skating after the 1988 Olympics. He skated with more skill than ever. In 1991, he set a new world record in the 500-meter race.

Dan Jansen went to the 1992 Olympics in France full of hope. Once again, he was the favorite to win the 500-meter race. He was the best in the world. No matter how many races you win, though, the Olympics are still the most important and most watched sports events in the world. Dan Jansen expected to win.

But something went wrong. That night, he did not skate like the Dan Jansen people knew. He had lost his edge. "When I crossed the line, I didn't have to look at my time," he said. "I knew it wouldn't be good enough for a gold. Perhaps not even for a medal."

Dan Jansen finished fourth in the 500-meter race. "As far as I was concerned, it might as well have been forty-fourth," he said. His loss crushed him. He went into hiding.

But Dan Jansen could not afford to go into a corner and brood. Three days later, he was to race the 1,000 meters. In that race, Dan did even worse. He finished 26th. Why? Today, Dan Jansen says he was not prepared to win. He didn't have the heart. Once again, U.S. hopes of gold in men's speed skating were dashed.

Dan Jansen doesn't have it, his critics said. He's not tough enough. Push him, and he falls. During both Olympics, Dan was supposed to win. Both times he had failed. He had bitterly disappointed himself. He had disappointed his fans.

But Dan Jansen recovered.

In the two years after the disaster in France, two wonderful things happened to Dan. He got married—and he and his wife, Robin, had a baby. They named her Janie, for Dan's sister.

But now it was 1994. It was time for the Olympics in Norway. Once again, the pressure was on. This was Dan Jansen's last Olympics. Would he choke again? Once again, he was skating in the 500-meter race. Once again, his fellow skaters expected him to win. But the critics told fans not to expect too much. Dan Jansen doesn't have what it takes, they said. He may be a fine skater, but he can't take the pressure of the Olympics. He's not a real world champion.

Dan Jansen knew what people were saying about him. He stood there waiting, tense and determined. The gun cracked for the start of the 500-meter race. Dan was off like a shot. Dan's wife, Robin, was in the stands. She was holding their baby, Janie. It was six years to the day that Jane had died.

Robin cheered him from the stands. "I thought he looked great," she said. Finally, it looked as if Dan Jansen's nightmare would be over. Then, on the last turn, the ice flew. Once again, Dan Jansen spun to the ground. Once again, he had fallen. Robin turned to her mother. "I can't believe this is happening again!" she screamed. Dan Jansen got up and began skating again. He finished eighth.

The speed skater that many call the best in history had one race left in his Olympic career. "This is my last shot," he told his family. "I want you to promise me that you're going to go out there and have fun. That's exactly what I plan to do."

Dan Jansen put on his skintight blue and red skating outfit. He fit his goggles to his eyes. He tightened his laces. Then he skated to the starting line. He thought about his sister Jane. He thought about his baby, Janie. He thought about his family rooting for him. He thought of the thousands of people around the world who were hoping he would put the past behind him and win. And then the gun went off.

Dan felt a jolt of energy in his legs. He began skating strongly, smoothly. The world was blank except for the motion of his skates. Then, on the second-to-last turn, he slipped. His hand shot to the ice. The people watching gasped. Would Dan Jansen choke again?

Don't panic, he remembered thinking. He straightened. He came out of it. Then he began to skate again, as he had never skated in his life. Dan Jansen crossed the finish line without a fall.

"My first thought when I crossed the line was, That's a medal," he wrote. He pulled off the hood of his uniform. Then he turned to look at the time. It flashed on the board.

1:12.43!

It was the fastest time Dan Jansen had ever skated the 1,000-meter race. And next to that time were the letters WR. Dan Jansen had set a new world record in the 1,000-meter race. Dan raised his arms and shut his eyes. He had done it.

The crowd roared. The champion who had won their hearts with his terrible troubles had won the race of his life. With tears of joy in his eyes, he skated over to where his wife and tiny daughter sat.

Suddenly he saw that his wife was passing baby Janie down through the rows of people. A guard handed Janie to her father. With Janie in his arms, Dan Jansen skated his victory lap. Across the stadium, and around the world, people cheered and cried. Finally, Dan Jansen had kept his promise. He'd won one for his sister Jane.

Think About It

1. Why did the ABC announcer say that the eyes of the world were on Dan Jansen at the 1988 Olympics?

2. Why was Dan Jansen known as the man who "choked" when he got to the Olympics?

3. Have you ever done something badly because you were troubled? Describe what happened.

Before You Read

One day, Jacob gets a letter from a long-lost love. In this story, the letter sends him on a journey he will never forget.

The Smell of Flowers

121 Mercy Lane
Sand Lakes, Ohio

Dear Jacob,

I don't know if I should be writing this. I don't know if you even live in Palmer now. You could be living in Alaska, as you said you would someday. But I had to try.

It's been so many years. Even so, I never forgot you. Not once. Do you remember the last time I saw you? When I told you I had to stop seeing you? I have never forgotten the look on your face. All the light seemed to go out of your eyes. I was so young! I didn't know I could say no to my parents. Then I left Palmer, to go to school. It's all a blur to me now, all of it. I graduated. I got married to the man my parents wanted me to marry. He was a fine man. We had two children. Life was just as my parents told me it would be, fine. A fine husband. A fine life.

Well, my children are grown. My husband died last year. Sad to say, I miss him but I miss you more. Isn't that odd? Will you write and tell me how you are?

Yours,
Janine

• • •

The old man read the letter again, for the third time. *Janine,* he thought. *Janine with the shy smile and the dark eyes. Janine. She broke my heart.* He sighed and looked down the prairie that swept away from his house. It was odd, he thought. He had been away from his home town, Palmer for years. He had left, just after Janine did. He had gone to Alaska, just as he'd told her he would. He had opened a store. Soon he had several stores. Never married, never had children. He never could get over Janine.

And now here she was writing to him, almost as if she'd known he had finally come back to Palmer. It was a sign, he thought. And yet, even after all these years, his memories were bitter. Janine's parents looking down at him, telling her he would never amount to anything. The shame he felt. The disappointment when Janine chose her parents over him.

He sat back, looking out at the prairie without seeing it, and a sudden gust of wind came up. It lifted the letter from his lap. The piece of paper sailed into the fields. Jacob ran, scrambling after it as fast as he could move. In that instant, he knew what he wanted. He ran faster. The letter blew down the fields until it was out of sight. He stood there, watching its flight, and felt a longing that surprised him. I didn't even look at the return address, he thought. But I will find her, he thought. I will.

Jacob set about this new task as he did any job. He sat down. He wrote out his plan. Find her family. Find her friends.

"Janine Wyant? Haven't talked to her in years. Think she married a man named Olson. Or was it Nelson? Sorry. Can't help you," said one childhood friend."Sure, she got married right here. Can't remember much about the man now, but they moved to Ohio. Or was it Iowa?" said another old family friend.

"Janine. Sure was pretty. Nope. Haven't talked to anyone in that family in years. Didn't something happen to them? Lose the business or something?"

No one, it seemed, had kept in touch. Jacob kept searching. He found the record of the wedding. The name was Olson. He found the family in a nearby county.

"Janine? Kinda lost track of her, since Ray died. Think she moved," said a cousin of Janine's dead husband.

"Where did they live before?" Jacob asked.

"Let's see—out in Ohio. Somewhere in Ohio. Sand something."

Jacob pored over a map of Ohio. Sandusky? Maybe. But maybe not. Sand Lakes? Sand Point? The next day, Jacob was on his way to Ohio. An hour after he left, the mail came. In the mail was a letter from Janine. It had been three months since her first letter.

• • •

121 Mercy Lane
Sand Lakes, Ohio

Dear Jacob,

You either don't live there, or you don't care. Even so, it felt comfortable writing you, so I'm going to write you again. I feel the need. Maybe it's because I know I won't hear from you.

I didn't tell you in my last letter, but I've been sick. I guess that was why I wrote. I've been thinking about the past. I have cancer. It's been hard. I don't much look like myself anymore (I couldn't tell you that in my first letter), and I'm tired most days.

Lately I've been thinking more about our first days together. The flowers you tried to pick by the bank, and how you lost your footing and fell into the river.

I guess it's better you never wrote back or came to see me. I'm not the same anymore. Sometimes it's better to live with the way things were.

Yours,
Janine

• • •

Jacob felt the sun warm his arm resting on the car window. He was getting close to Sand Lakes. Blue sky, the breath of spring in the air. It reminded him of the time he tried to pick flowers for Janine on the riverbank, and fell in to the river. She had tried not to laugh, but her dark eyes had done it for her. He smiled to himself, thinking of that day and that sparkling girl.

He'd had no luck in Sandusky. He had decided to keep going. Sand Lakes was a town a lot like Palmer. It was surrounded by fields, and it had a small downtown. Jacob found a phone booth. He looked up Janine. No listing. He closed the book and closed his eyes. Then he leaned back against the telephone booth. Once more, nothing. Well, might as well try the gas station.

"Ever heard of an Olson family around here?" he asked a man pumping gas.

The man at the other pump nodded. He pointed with the gas nozzle. "Right over there. Not a lot of people in this town."

The house was an old two-story building. Paint peeling. Garden left to itself, mostly. He almost turned back. Then he shrugged and walked up to the front door. The place looked unwelcoming, as if no one inside much cared what the world thought. He rang the doorbell. No one answered. He rang again. He waited, rang one last time, prepared to leave. He was down the steps when the door opened.

From the partly opened door, he saw a woman look out. She was old—as old as me, he thought to himself. Her face had the look of someone who never went outside, he thought as he went back up the walk. No Janine there.

As he got nearer, she looked at him closely. "Yes?" she said softly, as if it were an effort.

"I'm looking for an old friend—" he started to say as she moved into the sunlight. He saw dark eyes. "Janine?"

"Jacob," she said, and he could tell the effort it cost her.

"Janine? Is it you?"

Suddenly, she began to laugh, that rich, deep laugh he remembered. "Well, who else would it be?" she said.

His arms went around her thin, frail body. He tried to see the Janine of so many years ago. Somewhere in those fragile bones was the Janine he remembered.

"It would be you," he said, smelling the flowers in her hair, the smell of flowers on a riverbank fifty years ago. "It would be you."

"And you," she said. Her voice was muffled. She was surprised at how fast her heart was pounding. He was the same boy she remembered. Older. Grayer. Thinner. Like me. But it felt comfortable in his arms. Like they belonged together. Funny, she thought. Here they were, hours from Palmer, but standing there with Jacob, it felt like she had come home.

Think About It

1. Why did Janine write the letters to Jacob?
2. As Janine and Jacob get to know one another again, what do you think will happen to them?
3. Have you ever lost contact with a friend and then found that friend again? Explain how you felt.

Before You Read
Sarah has searched for Bigfoot for years. What she finally finds in the mountains is not what she expected.

The Beast in the Bush

Even now, my hands are shaking. It is hard to write. But I must put down everything I saw and did, or I will forget. Even so, I am afraid that others will not believe it. What I saw was so strange—but I must start at the beginning.

My name is Sarah Licht. I live in the Blue Mountains in Washington State. I have lived here all my life. In this part of the country, you grow used to hearing stories about Bigfoot. My father spent most of his spare time searching for Bigfoot. He wasn't the only one. Many people around here are sure that somewhere in these mountains, they will find the beast.

Some people, like my dad, came close—really close. My dad told me a story of being in the mountains when he smelled a bad odor. It made him gag. He looked to see where the smell was coming from. Then he heard a scream. It made the hairs on the back of his neck stand up, he said. The scream was high. It was a screech like nothing on earth. Then he saw fur moving quickly. Soon the smell was gone. My father was sure he had seen, heard—and smelled—Bigfoot.

Finding Bigfoot has been a hobby around here for many years. It began with the Native Americans who lived here hundreds of years ago. They called the strange hairy beast they saw Sasquatch (sas-kwoch).

Since then, hundreds of people have said that they have seen Bigfoot. Everyone described Bigfoot as huge—eight or nine feet tall. He was covered with black or dark brown hair. Some said the beast was gentle. Others weren't so sure.

After my dad saw Bigfoot, though, finding the beast was all he cared about. As soon as he finished work, he'd be off in the woods. He always took his rifle with him. When he saw my wide eyes, he tried to explain. "Even if Bigfoot is gentle," he said, "there are plenty of other things in the woods, Sarah." He paused. "Plenty of things that could tear a man to pieces."

A couple of times he came back and his eyes were wild. He never spoke of his hunt. While I was growing up, I watched him, and I got interested in the search for Bigfoot. I began reading everything I could find about it.

I read that Bigfoot had not just been seen in the Blue Mountains. Others said that they had seen Bigfoot in Oregon. There were sightings in California. But still, no one had been able to get more than a footprint. And some of those footprints seemed to be suspect.

One day I asked my dad if I could go along with him. He shook his head violently. "No!" he shouted. I took a step backward. His voice was so rough. He calmed down. "No, Sarah. You don't know what you're asking. I have seen things. . . . Whatever you have heard, that is no gentle beast out there."

"But why are you so set on finding it, if it's so dangerous?" I asked him.

He only shook his head. "I don't know. I somehow feel I was meant to find Bigfoot. I can't explain it."

He didn't take me with him. But not long after that, Dad went off again one Saturday morning to look. He never came home. Our neighbors all searched for him.

Three days later, two grim-faced men came to the door. They had their hats in their hands. One man, Jim Peters, wouldn't look at me or my mother. I watched his rough hands work over the beaten-down brim of his hat. The man with him, Jacob Bender, cleared his throat.

"Mrs. Licht?"

"Yes?" asked my mother. She was pale. She knew.

"We have some bad news." Jacob Bender cleared his throat again. "We found Sam. I'm sorry. He—"

My mother nodded quickly and put her hand over her eyes. "I know," she said. "I know. He's dead. Where did you find him?"

"Over there, way back by Boon Creek," Jim Peters said, pointing far into the mountains. "We told the others. They're bringing him down now."

My mother nodded again. Her face was still and white. She groped for a chair and sat down. "It was that beast," she said flatly. "That Bigfoot."

The men looked quickly at each other. Then Jim Peters spoke. "We got to go now, Mrs. Licht. Take care."

They still talk about what my father's body looked like when they brought it down from the mountain. He had a look on his face, they said. As if he'd been scared to death. There was one long, terrible gash across his chest. It had killed him.

The other thing people talked about was the place they'd found him. Like a den, almost, they said. A bed with fresh pine needles. Bones from some half-eaten animal around. Like somebody—or something—lived there.

• • •

My mother never got over my father's death. Neither did I. My reaction was different from hers, though. I wanted to find out more. She never wanted to

hear about the mountains again. I never saw her eyes wander up there after that day. It was as if the mountains no longer existed for her.

I never told her where I was going, on those long walks. I didn't want her to know.

During the next few years, I came close to finding Bigfoot. Once I heard the scream. Another time, I saw a footprint that was at least twenty inches long. It looked just like a person's, but twice the size.

Finally, yesterday something happened. It was a Saturday. I had packed a lunch in my backpack, stuck in my camera, and headed off. Once again, I was headed for Boon Creek.

That was usually where I went. That was where my father had died. It was where I would find answers, I was sure. It was an overcast day. Once again, I went to the place where they had found my father.

The wind was blowing through the clearing. Some of the bones were still there, scattered on the ground. The pine needle bed was long gone. I sat on the ground, ate lunch, and thought about where to go next. Behind me, I heard a branch snap heavily.

I whipped my head around. All was silent. But over there, where I had heard the sound, was a path I had not seen before. Branches were broken on the ground.

Quietly, I rose. I walked toward the path. The wind began whipping the pine trees. The path was narrow through the trees. I smelled the fresh smell of the pine needles as they scratched my face.

The path was strange. Small trees were hacked off. The path was strewn with broken branches. I made my way slowly, watchfully. The wind was picking up. It moaned. I heard the creak of branches rubbing together. For about an hour, I followed the path. Then I came to a clearing. When I saw it, I took a quick breath.

It looked like the clearing where my father had been killed. In one corner, a bed of pine needles. In another, fresh bones from some half-eaten animal. Then I smelled it. A smell like death. It hit my nose. I gagged and closed my eyes. I heard breathing and saw a quick movement to the right. I whipped my head around. Nothing.

Suddenly, the smell was overpowering. Something—an arm, I thought—circled my neck. It squeezed. I began to choke. I heard that high scream, like all the fury of the world in a voice. Then I blacked out.

When I woke up, the beast was sitting there staring at me. Bigfoot. It was huge and covered with dark brown fur. Its head looked like an ape's head. It was just sitting there, perfectly still. I stared back. It had an odd look in its eyes—almost human, I thought. And yet, not long ago, this beast had tried to choke the life from me.

The creature just sat there. Then I heard another sound behind me. Startled, I realized that someone was moaning. Slowly, keeping my eyes on Bigfoot, I moved so I could find the source of the sound. Behind me was a man. He was flat out on the ground. His hair hung long down his back. His dark beard reached the middle of his chest. He wore rags. In his fist was a knife.

While I watched, he moaned again. Suddenly, I was frozen with fear and confusion. Who was the evil one here? Was it the man, or Bigfoot? Whose arm had been around my neck, ready to break it?

The man's eyes snapped open. He focused on me, narrowly. He bared his teeth. As he tried to rise, he brought up his knife. Bigfoot rose. He walked over to the man. With one sweep of his arm, he knocked the knife from the man's hand. Then he walked back to where he had been sitting.

The man began to recover. He scrambled for his knife. With a yell, he launched himself at the hairy creature. Bigfoot screamed that high-pitched scream. He swatted at the man's hand. The man brought his hand back to plunge the knife into Bigfoot's chest.

Bigfoot caught his arm. They fell to the ground, fighting. The battled raged. Bigfoot grabbed the man and threw him across the clearing.

The man scrambled up and launched himself at Bigfoot. They struggled and broke apart. Then the man came at him again.

Shaken, I backed away as the sounds grew fiercer in the clearing. Suddenly, I lost my nerve. Without a look back, I picked myself up and began running. Behind me, I heard the sounds of battle. Roars and screams followed me down the mountain.

And now I sit writing this. I don't exactly understand what happened. I know that everything I thought was wrong. Bigfoot was no monster. A man was the monster.

Think About It

1. How did Sarah's and her mother's reactions to her father's death differ?
2. In view of Sarah's experience, how do you think her father died?
3. Do you agree with Sarah when she says "a man was the monster" at the end of the story? Why or why not?

Before You Read
César Chávez had the fire of justice in his eyes. These news articles describe how Chávez got farm workers the respect and rights that they deserved.

"We Have the Justice of Our Cause"

Chávez Ends Fast

DELANO, CALIFORNIA, March 10, 1968—Weak and beaming with happiness, labor leader César Chávez ended his fast today. He had not eaten for 25 days.

"Our struggle is not easy," said Reverend Jim Drake. He read the words Chávez had written. Chávez was too weak to speak. "But we have something the rich do not own. We have our own bodies and spirits. And we have the justice of our cause as our weapon."

While more than 4,000 people watched, Senator Robert Kennedy handed Chávez a piece of bread to break his fast. Then Kennedy spoke. "The world must know that the migrant farm worker, the Mexican American, is coming into his own right."

In September, 1965, grape pickers went on strike. Chávez's union, the United Farm Workers (UFW), decided to join the strike. By the next year, it was clear that the grape pickers needed more than a strike to win.

Chávez targeted grape growers for a boycott. The growers switched labels with other companies. Chávez decided there was only one way to get around that. He called for a boycott of all California grapes.

The boycott had a big effect on California grape sales. Sales went down, growers say. This time, however, the strike was to stop the violence of his own workers. Fights had broken out on picket lines. Chávez told his members the violence had to stop. To make his point, he began his hunger strike. Chávez lost 35 pounds.

Whether he would be able to lead his farm workers to a new contract was still not clear, though. The boycott and strike were already three years old.

Farm Workers Claim Victory

DELANO, CALIFORNIA , July 29, 1970—Today, California's largest grape growers ended the strike that has crippled them for five years. They announced they would sign contracts with César Chávez's group, the United Farm Workers.

"Today, we have won," said a smiling Chávez.

Union Leader Chávez Dead at 66

DELANO, CALIFORNIA, April 23, 1993—César Chávez, the union leader, died today. He was 66.

Chávez was hailed as a leader of the farm workers he devoted his life to. "Without him, there would be nothing for us," said one worker. "He gave his life for us."

Chávez worked hard to get better wages and working conditions for farm workers. Chávez ran a successful grape boycott in the late 1960s. He also ran boycotts of wine and lettuce. The boycotts put pressure on growers. The United Farm Workers (UFW) wanted growers to sign contracts with them.

By 1972, the UFW had 60,000 members. In the 1970s, another union, the Teamsters Union, also tried to organize farm workers. In 1977, the two unions reached an agreement. The UFW would organize field workers.

The Teamsters would organize truck drivers and people who worked in canning factories.

In the 1980s, the UFW boycotted table grapes. The union was trying to get growers to stop using pesticides. The chemicals, the union said, were hurting the workers' health. When Chávez died, the UFW had about 100,000 members.

Chávez was the son of farm workers. He was born in Yuma, Arizona, in 1927. During the Great Depression, his family lost their farm. When they could not pay the taxes on the land, it was sold at an auction. They moved to California. Chávez was ten years old.

The Chávez family was not alone. More than 300,000 hungry people also headed for California. There, they hoped to find work. However, there was little work in California. People were paid pennies to work on the farms.

Chávez's father, Librado, joined a union that was trying to organize the farm workers. Then his father was hurt in a car wreck. César Chávez was in eighth grade. The family needed help to make a living. Chávez left school to work in the fields full-time.

In 1952, Chávez met Fred Ross. Ross was looking for people to help him organize Mexican Americans in California. After meeting Chávez, Ross wrote in his diary, "I think I've found the guy I am looking for."

Chávez began to spend all his spare time helping his people. He worked nights to register Mexican Americans to vote. Soon he had a job working for the Community Service Organization (CSO). The CSO worked for Mexican Americans in California.

For Chávez, the most important thing was fair treatment for farm workers. He learned that growers were hiring Mexicans to come across the border and work. They were paid very poor wages. Mexican Americans were forced out of jobs.

Chávez won the fight to stop hiring foreign workers. Mexican Americans were then able to get jobs. The next hurdle was harder. The real need farm workers had, he said, was for a union. That was the only way that they could get paid a fair wage. It was the only way they could get respect.

In 1965 a new union was formed. The new union was called the National Farm Workers Association (NFWA). It had its first strike. They struck a company that grew roses. The workers were to be paid $9 for every 1,000 rose plants they spliced. To splice a rose bush, workers made a tiny cut in the plant. Then they put a tiny rosebud into the cut. Instead of getting $9, though, the workers brought in to replace the strikers were only getting $6.50. After four days, the company gave in to the strike. The new workers it had hired could not do the job. The company agreed to pay the NFWA workers what it had said it would. The strike got the attention of other farm workers. Many joined the NFWA.

That same year, 1965, the UFW began the grape boycott. The grape boycott grabbed the country's attention. From that time, César Chávez became known as the man who devoted his life to his people.

Think About It

1. Why did César Chávez want to help the farm workers?
2. Why did Chávez boycott California grapes?
3. Do you think a boycott is ever right? Explain.

Before You Read

Is there a sport that you like? This poem was written by a basketball fan who finds a number of things she likes about basketball.

My Basketball

Bobbi Katz

I love the sound of it.
Its thump, thud, thud,
when
I
dribble
down
the
court.
I love the sting of it,
landing in my hands
on a cool, clean pass.
But most of all,
I love the way it whispers
"Yes!"
rising in a perfect arc
and dropping through
the
hoop.
And in that moment
I seem to hear it say,

"We might make it all the way—
all the way
through school
and then
the NBA!"

Think About it

1. What are two things that the poet loves about basketball?
2. How do you think the poet feels when she plays the game?
3. Name two things that you enjoy about a sport. Make sure your explanation is very specific.

Before You Read

The band went to New York to make it big. But are they good enough? In his journal, the band leader records their ups and downs.

Music to Beat New York By

July 9

Today was probably the worst. We've been in New York City five months now. Money is running low. Carrot is talking about packing up and heading back to Cincinnati. It was all I could do to keep him from splitting.

July 15

Great day today. We found a warehouse where we can practice. It's in the meat packing part of the city. It's pretty weird at night. There are some artists down there, and some meat lockers. Strange to think of all that meat hanging below us while we play.

July 16

Great practice today. Lemmy was amazing. The rest of us just stood there and stopped playing, to listen to him. The sound kind of soared out of his guitar. You can't follow it. You just have to listen. I watched Carrot watching. He was trying to pick it up on his instrument. He couldn't do it. I watched his face get all mad. He seems to think Lemmy is showing off. I know better. When Lemmy gets like that, he's not thinking of anything but the music. But you can't tell Carrot that. The guy is so hard to deal with sometimes. Maybe I should have let him go when he wanted.

September 1

It's getting harder to keep the band together. We haven't had a real gig in about a month. Just this fill-in stuff. We've gone through all our money. Jeff and Lemmy took second jobs. Whatever else you can say about this place, it sure is expensive.

October 10

The weather is getting cooler. Dates are starting to pick up. A while back we opened for a local band, The Japes. They've got a big following. Their music is also sort of like ours. They're a little rougher, but still, we sort of click together. Maybe we can open for them again.

October 11

I was so wrong. Stupid, greedy people. The Japes got hired to come back, and when I asked about opening for them again, they kind of looked away. I know it's not that we're no good. It's worse than that. They think we're better than they are. Better to keep us in our place. No shows now for 3 weeks. Once again, I gotta keep the troops together. It's getting old. For some reason, this latest thing got to me. I mean, would it have killed them to give us a break? What a crummy city.

October 12

Victory, of sorts. Great. We get to open for a band that hates us. But after The Japes blew us off, the manager at Rat Time called. They want us back. Yes! Can't wait to see the faces on those punks when they find out.

October 17

So the manager of the place comes over to me today after our set. He puts his arm around my shoulder. "So," he says, "you like it here? We're getting a good response to you. People are coming in just to hear you.

I got a deal for you. You and The Japes switch off. One night you take the lead. The other night they do." "Have you talked to them yet?" I asked. I couldn't stop grinning. I didn't want to, but I couldn't stop. "No," the guy shakes his head. "Not yet. I wanted to run it by you first. Raise OK?" he says. He's pleased with himself. Expecting me to get on my back and kick my legs in the air. Even though the money's still not enough to live on, I'm supposed to be thrilled. Problem is, I am.

November 5

The band is together. Getting that regular starting gig was it. Having someone else think you're good is what it takes. You can think it all you want. Until someone else agrees with you, what you think doesn't matter.

November 15

Carrot is getting weird again. He's so jealous of Lemmy. He can't understand that for a lot of people, he—Carrot—is the band. That weird, high voice of his echoes in people's heads. They remember him—probably his hair. It is hard to forget.

November 17

Carrot left today. Packed up when we were gone during the day and took off. I'm beyond angry. He could mess up everything for us. At least now I don't have to spend my time getting him through his moods. Still, though, I have to admit that I'm more than just mad. He hurt my feelings.

November 30

Lost the Rat Time gig. Said it was time for something new. We were sounding tired. I know that's not it. It's that Carrot left. He had more of a following than I thought. Lemmy's talking about leaving now, too. I have to do something.

December 5

Found a great singer. Her name is Julie. Great looking. Long white-blond hair with black eyes. Her voice is different. Sometimes the voice sounds like honey. Other times, it sounds like metal on a grater.

December 15

It's late, real late, for holiday gigs. Last-minute things happen, though. So, to make a long story short—we ended up at Eno, one of the hottest clubs in town. Julie was an instant hit. I knew I was right about her. Looks like she's mooning over Lemmy. He hasn't a clue, as usual. Sam would go for her, I think. But she's not interested in him. Or me, either.

December 20

Big news. A record company sent someone to hear us. He came up after the show. He wanted to know who represented us. We gave him a demo tape. He said he'd get back to us after the holidays. This could be it.

December 25

Christmas. We're all feeling pretty good these days. I'm a little worried about Sam, though. He's so stuck on Julie. He wrote her a song and played it. He asked her to listen to it. She told him she couldn't. She was going out for Christmas dinner with some guy she'd met. So Sam played it for us anyway. It was a love song, written to Julie. That was clear. I think she knew it. That was why she left. It's not that she's mean. She just doesn't feel that way about him. Why is it always these kind of things that bands have to deal with? Why can't people just play and forget the jealousy and the fights?

December 27

Big fight tonight. Sam was going to tell Julie how he felt about her tonight. No matter what anyone said.

He told her. We were in another part of the room, but we saw him talking to her. He finished. Then she gave him this look. He looked back at her like a wounded deer and blew out. Hasn't been back since. Meanwhile, Lemmy is still about as clueless as it gets. Sits in the corner with his guitar. Julie could maybe get his attention by sitting on the guitar. That's the only way, though.

January 19

The record company called yesterday. Said the label was interested in the band. Could we come in and play? Of course, at this point Sam is still gone. And Julie is still running after Lemmy. Lemmy, of course, is still in the corner with his guitar. Thank goodness for Bosco. Bosco is still on drums. Mr. Reliable. I asked the record company to give me a week. We set up the session for the end of next week. Finding Sam will be the number-one job.

January 22

No word on Sam. The band doesn't sound the same without him. There's something wrong. We still have all our gigs, but it isn't the sound the record guys heard. We gotta find him. I've checked with everyone he knows. I even put ads on bulletin boards. I'm starting tomorrow to check places where he's done part-time work.

January 24

Found him. He was loading trucks. Still nursing his hurt pride, like some dumb puppy. I told him about the date with the record label. That was all it took. He's back. And two days from now, we're on.

January 26

Today was incredible. It's the reason we came to New York. The record label had a bunch of suits in to watch us.

That made me nervous. This is not suit music. But they liked it anyhow. You can feel when it's going well. You can see it. They smile, they tap feet. All that stuff. Afterward, they sat down with us. Told us it looked good. Asked about our manager. The record guy frowned when he heard I was the manager. He scribbled the name of a guy I've heard of. He told me to call and get a real manager. Afterward, we went out to celebrate. Once again, it was Julie, tossing her hair at Lemmy. Sam was staring at Julie with hope in his eyes. And Lemmy. You gotta laugh. He sits there, looking at his rice pudding. The guy is unreal. But the good news got us all going. Nobody's slamming out tonight. Everything is good. Really, really good.

September 15

Can't believe I haven't written for so long. So much has been happening, though. We got a record contract in LA and a new manager. A real manager, who knows how to get real jobs. Our first CD will be out in three months. And the most unbelievable change is Sam and Julie. Right now they're sitting in a corner, holding hands again. They say you never know what's going to happen to you in New York. They got that right. But once in a while, I guess, it's better than you ever thought it could be.

Think About It

1. Why did the band go to New York City?
2. Why did the band start to become successful?
3. If you were the band leader, what advice would you give other bands that want to become successful?

Before You Read

When Van dreams, he hears the gunfire in Cambodia. He feels the terror. He hears his mother scream. Van must know: Is his mother still alive?

Dream of the Killing Fields

Van bolted upright in bed. "Mama!" he screamed. He was covered in sweat. Once again, the dream. He was back in Cambodia. He was running and running, gasping for breath. Behind him he could hear machine-gun fire. People were falling all around him. Still he kept running and crying. His mother looked at him. Her face was wild. "Run, Van! Run!" she screamed.

"Was that you again last night?" his friend Heng said the next morning. He stood in the kitchen, frying rice. It crackled in the pan.

"Yeah," Van said. He sat in the kitchen, rubbing his eyes. He knew he looked as bad as he felt. "I can't get away from the dream. You know the one."

Heng nodded. He turned back to his rice.

"I start running from those men. I can see their faces. I will never forget their faces. They are the ones who beat me. They beat my sister. They forced us into those camps. They dragged people out and just shot them for no reason. No reason . . ."

Heng nodded patiently. "I know, Van. I know. I was there. I am Cambodian, too. Remember? There is no part of 1975 that I will ever forget. The year the Communists marched in and took over or 1977, when the food ran out. The way the Communists made us work in the rice fields fifteen hours a day. And then they took all the rice. And what did they give us? A cob of corn for the day. That's it. A cob of corn. And later, not even that. A little bit of rice for twenty, thirty people." Heng looked at Van. "Who could forget? But when you dream every night, it must be worse."

"It is," Van said. He drank the sweet, thick coffee Heng handed him. "I am never free. It is as if my dreams are telling me something." He looked at Heng. "You know what I think they are saying? They are telling me to find my mother."

Heng snorted and brought the fried rice to the table. "Find your mother? How exactly do you expect to begin? She may have come here, to California. Not very likely. There are so many other places she could be. She could have stayed in Cambodia." He paused. "Or—"

"I know what you are going to say," Van said. He was tired. "You're going to say she could be dead. I know all that. But I also know that until I find her, I will get no rest. I've been thinking about it. I need a plan."

Heng dug into his breakfast. He shrugged. "So go ahead and look for your mother. Just don't expect to find much."

"It is something I must do," Van said. He finished the rice and washed the dishes. Then he left the apartment. The San Francisco air was chilly. He turned up his collar against the cold. Brave words, Van thought. But what do I do? Where do I go? He turned into the restaurant where he worked as a busboy. Samol, another Cambodian refugee, sat on a stool. His legs were up on the sink. His head was stuck in a copy of a Cambodian newspaper.

"Good morning," Van said to him. Samol grunted. Van turned to his work. His mind was still busy with its puzzle. How to find his mother? For a moment, he was back in Cambodia as a child. He was in his mother's arms.

She hugged him. She looked down on him with a smile that had all the love in the world in it. She hummed a song to him. Van looked down quickly so no one could see the tears forming in his eyes.

During the next week, the nightmares returned every night. During the day, Van tried to come up with ideas on where to find his mother. But he was so tired from not sleeping, he couldn't think.

The dream came again that night. In the morning, Van dragged himself in to work. Once again, Samol read his paper and grunted. Van sat next to him, utterly worn out. He found himself staring at the front page of the Cambodian newspaper. Suddenly, he had an idea.

After work, he hurried to the newspaper office. He barely said hello before telling his story. "Can you help me?" he asked. "A good story, isn't it? Could you write it?"

The woman at the desk looked at him sadly. She had heard it before. "It's not news," she said. "I'm sorry."

Van looked at her. He looked down, quickly. He didn't want her to see his tears. He blinked his eyes to clear them. Van's gaze dropped to the newspaper on the desk. His eyes rested on an ad with the smiling face of a car salesman."What about an ad?" he asked eagerly.

"An ad." The woman was thoughtful. "I never thought of that. Of course, it costs a lot of money. And it's only one newspaper. What if your mother is in Chicago?"

"How much is an ad this size?" Van asked, pointing to the car salesman.

"Well, let's see," the woman said, and walked to the back to get the cost sheet.

Van had not spent much of his money. He had always saved it. This, he thought, was because of what had happened to him. Money was one way of protecting yourself. Now, though, he had no more interest in saving.

At home, Van got out a photo of his mother. The photo was old. It had been hidden and handled so much, the edges were soft. The photo was bent. He looked at it. He saw his mother's smiling face. He tucked the photo in his pocket. He half ran to the newspaper office.

For a month, the readers of the *Cambodian Times* saw Van's mother smiling sweetly at them. "Attention!" the ad said. "Van Mao is looking for his mother, Meach Mao. Please call."

Van had no answer to his ad. Then he had no more money. On the day the last ad ran, Van went down to the newspaper office. "I am saving my money for more ads. But I also need the addresses of other Cambodian newspapers. Do you have them?"

The woman at the desk was by now quite taken by Van and his search. She gave him a list of Cambodian newspapers in the United States. That night, Van wrote to them, asking how much ads would cost.

The same day, Arthur Pok was sitting at his desk at the *San Francisco Examiner*. One of his jobs as a reporter was to keep up with the Cambodian community. He was Cambodian American. His parents spoke the language at home. Arthur knew enough of the Khmer language to read the paper. As he sipped his coffee, he looked again at the smiling face of Meach Mao. Every week for the last month he had gazed at her photo. Something about it touched him. Maybe it was her smile. Maybe it was the way the photo was creased. It looked as if it had been carried all the way from Cambodia.

Arthur made up his mind. He swung his legs to the ground and stood up. He stretched. Then he headed for the office of the *Cambodian Times*.

"So who is this Van Mao?" he asked the woman at the desk. He pointed to the ad.

She smiled at him. "Hello, Arthur. He's a very nice young man. Sad, though. He's so sad. Haunted, really. He was so excited when he put in the ad. So sure. Every week, when he heard nothing, he got sadder. It breaks my heart." She shook her head. "So many. So many dead. So many lost."

"Thanks," Arthur said. When he got back to the office, he called Van.

"Is this Van Mao?" he asked.

"Yes." Arthur could hear the eagerness in the voice. "And you are?"

"Arthur Pok. *San Francisco Examiner*. I understand you're looking for your mother."

"That's right," the voice said. "Have you heard? Do you know anything?"

Arthur sighed. "No, no. I know nothing. But I am interested in your story. The ad. Can I talk to you?"

"Yes. Yes. Of course. Right now?" Van asked, eager again.

Arthur laughed. "Well, I was thinking of tomorrow. What time is good for you?"

"I'm off work in the morning. Please come by. Nine. Please. I live at sixty Warner. You will come?"

"Yes," Arthur said. "I'll be there." He hung up, thinking about the ties between mother and son. The ties that last through war, across time, and around the world.

The next morning, Arthur was there at nine. "Come in, come in," Van said. Arthur took quick notes. Van looked tired. The apartment was tidy. It had very little in it. The picture was on the table.

"So, Van," he said, sitting down, "tell me about yourself."

Van took a deep breath and began.

That afternoon, a photographer from the newspaper came by. He took a picture of Van. Van stood straight. He held the photo in his hand. He looked ahead without a smile.

Arthur began to write. Something about Van's story had touched him. He wrote of Van's childhood in the killing fields of Cambodia. He wrote how the tears came to Van's eyes as he smoothed the picture and talked of his mother. Arthur finished the story and smiled. He knew it was good.

It was on the front page of the paper the next day. Someone at the wire service saw the story and put it on the wire. Van was overjoyed when Arthur explained this to him. "That means, Van, that newspapers everywhere will get this story. They'll get the picture, too. If your mother is in this country, I bet she will see this."

Arthur was right about one thing. People all over the country saw the story. They read about the Cambodian man's search for his mother. How he spent his savings on ads. How he heard nothing. Offers of help came from around the country. Some people sent money. Others sent information tips. A week after the story ran all over the country, Van stopped getting calls.

• • •

In Detroit, Meach Mao tiredly picked up the day's newspaper at the home where she worked as a housekeeper. The Roberts, the family she worked for, had not touched the paper. Meach wondered if they meant to read it. Then she shrugged. They must not. The paper was near the pile for recycling. As she put it in the pile, her eye caught something, a picture. Something looked familiar. She gasped. It was a picture of her.

Meach panicked. She could not read English. To her, the picture could mean only one thing. The men from Cambodia were looking for her. It wasn't over. The Communists were here. Still very scared, Meach sat down, holding the paper. She wished, more than anything, that she could read English. What was she to do? Was she safe here? Could they find her? And what about the Roberts, the family she worked for? Would they turn her in?

As she was trying to think, she heard the garage door opening. They were home. Quickly, Meach tore off the page. She crumpled it up. The door opened. Meach stuffed the wad of paper deep into a drawer.

• • •

Van was quieter than he used to be, Heng thought. He rarely spoke. His hopes of finding his mother had been so high. Suddenly Heng was angry. Angry at Van for being a dreamer. Angry at himself for caring. Mostly, he was angry at the things the world had done to them.

• • •

Five months later Meg Roberts reached deep into a drawer and found a crumpled ball of paper. Odd, Meg thought. What's this? She smoothed it out. Looking back at her was a picture of her housekeeper, Meach. The photo was old and scratched, but the picture was of a smiling, happy woman. Much younger than the Meach she knew. Much happier.

Meg jumped as she heard a sound behind her. Meach was standing there. Meg frowned. What was this? Was Meach wanted for something? Did she have some terrible secret? "What is it?" she asked Meach. "What's this about?" Meg asked. Meach ran.

Meg brought the paper to the light. Sitting down, she became lost in the story of a son's search for his mother.

"Meach!" Meg said, running for Meach's room. "You didn't read this! You won't believe it!"

Meach wasn't in her room. Puzzled, Meg ran with the story and the photo to the street. There was Meach, dragging her suitcase.

Meg ran to catch Meach. "Meach! It's not bad! It's good! It's your son—your son, Van! He's been looking for you! He wanted to find you. And now he has."

Slowly, as Meg spoke, the terror in Meach's face left. She put down the suitcase as Meg read the story. " . . . and still, Van searches. He says, the only thing he wants in life is to find his mother again."

Meach stood in the center of the road. Can this be true? she thought. Van. My Van. He escaped.

"We will call from the house," Meg said. "We'll find him. We'll fly you out. Don't worry."

Meg found Arthur Pok at the newspaper. She got Van's number. She called. And then, when a voice with an Asian accent answered, Meg gave the phone to Meach.

• • •

Two weeks later, Van stood at the airport. The door opened and people walked off the plane. Then a small, gray-haired woman appeared. She stopped just outside the door. Van ran to her. She cried. She heard him say, "Mama." And they were together again. Beyond the killing fields of Cambodia, safe and together.

Think About It

1. How did Van and his mother get separated?
2. Why did Van's mother crumple up the newspaper with her picture on it and hide it in a drawer?
3. If you were Van, would you have searched for your mother? Why or why not?

Before You Read
People said she would never make it as a ballet dancer. In this true story, Judith Jamison shows she has the spirit and strength to become whatever she wants.

No Ordinary Dancer

She was too tall, they said. Too African American. She might as well give up, the critics said. Judith Jamison would never make it as a ballet star. In life, though, Judith Jamison has had one strength. She has never listened to people who told her no.

Even as a child, she was different. "When I was six years old I was tall, lean, and long-legged," she says. "At ten I could walk down the street and see everybody's head. It's not that I felt especially tall. I was wondering when everybody else was going to catch up."

When she was six, Jamison began ballet lessons. Her teacher, Marion Cuyjet, was amazed. "I was so excited by her," she says. "All my husband and I talked about was Judi."

Jamison had a drive to be the best at sports, too. She remembers being put in the back row for a gymnastics show. She was put there, she felt, because she was African American. "I know I was good. There was no one on that stage doing this work better than I," Jamison said. "I was angry. But I knew even then how to direct my anger." She got on that stage and performed her heart out.

After high school, in 1965, Jamison went to college at Fisk University in Nashville, Tennessee. After three semesters there, Jamison realized that she had to dance. She moved to Philadelphia. There, she studied at the Philadelphia Dance Academy. It was also in Philadelphia that Agnes de Mille saw her dance. De Mille had the power make a dancer's career.

De Mille remembers when she first saw Jamison dance. "There were just the ordinary students," she later said. "Some good, some bad. With this one astonishing girl." De Mille worked for the American Ballet Theatre in New York City. She asked Jamison to go to New York. She wanted her to be in a new ballet. Jamison was thrilled. "I had pictures of the dancers all over my bedroom wall," she said.

Jamison danced the role. She was praised for her work. But when she tried to get work after the show closed, she failed. She was not the dancer most companies wanted. They wanted small, white women. Jamison was neither. But she didn't care. She never paid any attention to things she couldn't change, she said.

Jamison kept trying, but she couldn't get a job as a ballerina. Even so, Jamison stayed in New York. She was determined. She would dance. To support herself, she got a job as a clerk in an office.

Then she heard about a part for a ballet dancer on a TV show. She came to the audition wearing pink ballet shoes and a leotard. She wore the clothes of a classic ballerina. The other women wore stylish clothes. When Jamison began to dance, that was a diseaster too. It had been too long since she had danced. Her skills were rusty. she was asked to leave the audition. She left in tears.

Three days later, a man who had been there called her. He had liked what he had seen. The man was Alvin Ailey. He ran a dance group. He asked her to join. She said yes on the spot.

The dance company was the Alvin Ailey American Dance Theater. Together, Ailey and Jamison were a great team. He created brilliant dances. She danced them with a spirit that captured audiences.

The Alvin Ailey Dance Theater was well known in the United States. It was better known around the world. The company danced in Egypt. It danced in Europe. It danced in Africa. The company then danced in Spain, where they ran out of money. "We had faith in Alvin," Jamison said. "He believed his dancers had to keep going, no matter what."

In 1971, Alvin Ailey created the dance *Cry* for her. It was the dance she had been waiting for all her life. In a 16-minute dance, Ailey showed the history of African American women. Jamison made the dance a cry of love and courage. She stretched her 5'10" body across the stage. She made leaps others only dreamed of.

When she finished dancing *Cry* the first time, the people watching exploded in cheers. They knew that they were watching magic. "Judith Jamison is no ordinary dancer," wrote Clive Barnes, an important dance critic for *The New York Times*.

For Jamison, though, the most important critic was her grandmother. She was in the audience for opening night. "She hadn't seen me dance since I was eight years old, and I wanted to give the performance of my life," Jamison said. "I remember feeling and thinking that the dance was like a transfer of spirit from my grandmother to my mother to me."

Jamison became famous around the world. She posed for fashion magazines. She danced with the best-known dancers of her time. She danced in 70 different ballets for Alvin Ailey. She even took a chance on Broadway. She joined the cast of a musical called *Sophisticated Ladies*.

Alvin Ailey was hurt when she left. But Jamison couldn't stay in one place. "I wanted to try something else," Jamison said. "I gave up safety. I jumped into Broadway."

In 1988, she began her own dance group. She called it the Jamison Project. She also began helping Ailey. He was sick. His company needed help. Alvin Ailey died in 1989. Before he died, he asked Jamison to take over his company.

Jamison gave up her own company to run the Alvin Ailey American Dance Theater. "There was no way I could have refused Alvin," she said.

Jamison brought a new energy to the company. "I don't feel as though I'm standing in anyone's shoes," she said of Ailey. "I'm standing on Alvin's shoulders."

Along the way, Jamison worked incredibly hard. She learned her craft. She reached the top. But she did it her way. She turned what others thought were weaknesses into strengths. And she made the world change its ideas about what a dancer is. "Learn how to open your heart," she tells students. "Turn on your creativity. There's a light inside of you." That light shines from Judith Jamison.

Think About It

1. Why did critics say that Judith Jamison could not be a ballet star?
2. What qualities of Judith Jamison do you admire? Why?
3. Have you ever been told you couldn't do something? Explain.

Before You Read

One day, Frankie was hiking in the Amazon rain forest. Within months, she was dangerously thin. In this story, a young woman must learn how to save her own life.

The Curse of Being Too Thin

Frankie hadn't even noticed at first. She knew she was losing weight, but that was fine. She needed to lose a few pounds. Probably about 25, to be exact. But nothing had changed about the way she was eating. She felt good, she was stuffing herself—and she was losing weight. About two pounds a week, for about three months now.

By now, her clothes hung off her body. The word fat sounded good now. It sounded like praise. She had long ago given up trying to keep the clothes up with belts. She just wore loose dresses now. They hung off her body. Really, she thought, trying to keep down a crazed giggle, her clothes flapped around her.

It took Frankie a while to change from being delighted to being scared. She ate all the time and still got thinner. After a while, it stopped being fun. It became scary. No matter how much she ate, she lost weight. She ate everything. Before, she would have felt bad all day for eating a candy bar. Now, she ate a whole carton of triple fudge ice cream in one sitting. She kept candy bars by her bed. It didn't matter. It was as if she were eating rice cakes. The weight kept coming off.

Finally, she saw a doctor. It was not until she walked into his office that she saw how bad it was.

His eyes got wide. He tried not to show his surprise. "Well, Frankie. Been on a diet, yes?" He said it in that hearty doctor way. She hated that.

"No."

"No." He looked puzzled. Then uncomfortable. "Well, you certainly haven't been eating. Or have you been eating and then throwing up?"

"Neither."

Suddenly, he was all business. "Well, we need to get to the bottom of this." She felt relieved. Now the puzzle would be solved. The tests started. He took blood. He took X-rays. He poked and examined. By the end of the week, the doctor had found nothing. And Frankie had lost another two pounds.

"I have to be honest. I am concerned," he began. He was using that concerned-doctor voice she hated.

"So am I," she replied in her best patient voice.

He cleared his throat. "Well, perhaps there is something we overlooked. Has anything odd happened lately that you want to tell me about? Anything that may have caused this?"

She thought a moment. When had all this started? Was it—yes. "My vacation," she said. "I went to South America. And then all this began happening."

"South America." He looked at her. "And?"

"Well, that's all I know. I went to the Amazon rain forest. I hiked. I talked to people. I camped. And when I came home, I started losing weight."

"Did you feel sick?"

"No," she said impatiently. "Nothing like that. I—" She stopped suddenly. It was too weird to believe. No. That couldn't be it.

"What is it?" he asked.

"Nothing. Nothing."

They sat in silence for a moment. Then he stood up. "I will talk to a doctor I know. She studies tropical medicine. Perhaps she has an idea. I will call you. For now, you must keep eating. High-fat milkshakes. Steaks. Whatever sounds good to you. But keep eating." He walked her out.

As she was leaving Frankie thought about one of the villages she visited. We were hiking. We came to that village. There was an American student studying there. Frankie sat down on the steps of the building.

It was coming back to her. The village was very poor. Chickens were scratching in the dirt. Still, the people were nice. We stopped and had lunch in that small village. Everyone was eating together. Let's see, she said to herself. We sat down to eat. The food was disgusting. The plates were grimy. I told them I wasn't hungry. Then that old man's face got nasty. He spit out some words at me. Very angry—I remember that. But I wasn't going to eat that food. It was a filthy place. No way was I going to eat anything there. What did that old man say?

Frankie put her forehead in her hands. And the American? He had made some joke about the gods and a curse. But the old man wasn't laughing. A curse? She lifted her head. Right. A curse. She laughed, as if to try out the idea of a laugh. She shook her head to shake off the thoughts. Then she went home.

In a week, she was below 100 pounds. People tiptoed around her. She felt fine. She really did. But when she looked at herself, she saw a starving woman. It scared her. She stopped looking in the mirror.

That week, she decided to find the American student that was on the trip. It didn't take long to track him down. When he saw her, he was shocked.

She was strange-looking now. "Don't be frightened," she said quickly, putting up a skeletal hand. "I'm Frankie Post. We met in the Amazon. Remember the small village? I was hiking with a friend and stopped. You were studying there—"

"Yes," he said, nodding. "But I must ask. Are you all right?"

"That's why I'm here," she said. "May I sit down?"

"Of course," he said, ashamed. He cleared books from the sofa and made a space.

"It's about that village," she said, leaning forward. "That old man. Do you remember?"

He looked uncomfortable. "Yes."

"Do you remember why he was angry at me? Really angry? For not eating?"

"Oh, yes," he said. "I remember."

She looked at him. It was hard to read his face. It was as if he knew something he didn't want to tell her.

"Well?" she asked.

"I don't know. It's too strange."

She leaned forward. "Look at me. Since I got back from South America, I have lost fifty pounds. Fifty pounds! I've been eating like a horse, and look." She held up her arm. It looked like a stick.

"All right. I'll tell you what I know. But this is going to sound odd." Frankie nodded. "That group of people—it was strange that you hiked in there. Hardly anyone even knows they exist. I heard about them from a teacher I had. They are a small tribe. I was studying them. They were incredibly interesting, but I had to leave. I got scared."

"Scared? Why?"

"I said this would sound odd. They believe in spells. A kind of witchcraft, I guess. And that man you met—

he was the worst. He seemed to think everyone was out to get him. He had everyone in the village terrified. They thought he had powers. I saw things happen that I couldn't explain. Once, a wild pig ran by him. He lost his balance. Then he said some words and pointed at the pig. I swear I saw it disappear."

"When I wouldn't eat the food," she murmured. He nodded.

"That's what I was thinking. He was offended. If you wouldn't eat their food, maybe you shouldn't get nourishment from any food? I know it sounds crazy. But I saw things there that made no sense."

She nodded thoughtfully. "Well, I can believe anything now. The doctors can't find anything wrong. I feel fine. But if this keeps up, I'm going to be just bones in a few weeks. Do you have any ideas?"

He nodded. "I do. Go back. Find that man. Beg him. Bring him gifts. Do whatever you need to do to get his forgiveness. I think it's your only chance." He sat looking at her. "I can't believe I'm telling you these things. On the other hand, I can't believe what's happened to you."

"I know," she said. She stood up to go. "Thank you. Do you have any maps, by the way? I don't think I could find that place by myself."

He pulled out some torn pieces of paper and handed them to her. "They're not good maps, but they're all I have. And—good luck."

Frankie tried not to watch the glances she got on the plane trip to South America. Whoever said you can't be too thin never saw me, she thought. As soon as the plane landed, she set off for the village. First, there was a two-day boat ride up the river. The second night, she rested at a small inn and studied the maps. She had some idea of where to go. It looked like a three-day hike. She looked at her supplies. Plenty of high-energy food bars. A water purifier. Freeze-dried dinners. She was set.

The next day was hazy, warm, and moist. She knew the people who owned the inn were worried about her. They kept asking if she really wanted to go by herself. They looked at her carrying that heavy backpack. Then they looked at her sticklike legs and asked if she wanted to wait a week until they could spare a guide. A week! she thought. After I've lost another two pounds?

Strangely, she felt no fear. Overhead, the sound of thunder rolled lazily. Soon it was raining. She put her hood on and kept walking. The trail was clear, at least for now. And the maps were easy to read.

The rain kept falling. The water made the deep green leaves of the trees shine. Huge flowers of rich red hung over her head. She saw birds with rainbow colors. She almost stepped on snakes, slithering by her feet. She stopped for lunch in a clearing. There was a waterfall nearby. She breathed in the scent of flowers and rain. It is paradise here, she thought. Her happiness died the minute she thought of her search for the old man. What if he refused to help her? What if he were dead? What if she got lost? She quickly finished lunch and began walking.

That night she slept in her tent under the thick jungle trees. They were a shelter from the rain. Dinner was more energy bars. She couldn't get a fire started because it was so wet. She sat there, shivering. She was cold even in the warm air. That night she dreamed of the man. His mouth was an open cave. He had no teeth. He was laughing.

By the third day, she was wet through. She was tired from walking so far and so fast each day. But at the end of the third day, she took the last turn on the map that led to the village. Half an hour later, she saw signs of people. The path opened into the village soon after. She remembered it all. The huts made of broad jungle leaves. The dirt—now mud—ground around the huts. The smoke from the fires rising from the huts. The children who came up, curious, sucking on their fingers.

She was scared and relieved and hopeful, all at once. She had found the village. But she thought about that man. He seemed to have no good in him. As she stood there, people began to gather around her. She could not understand what people were saying. Someone gave a command to a child. He ran to a hut and went inside. Soon, a small woman came from the hut. She held out her hand. "I am Glee. I can speak English. Who are you?"

"I came here before. We had a meal together. I must speak to the old man who was at that meal." She said it all in a rush.

The woman listened politely. "Man? We have many men. Do you know his name?"

She shook her head. She took a deep breath. "I have come a long way. This man—I must see him. I think he—"

"He what?"

"I think I may have made him angry. I have to find him—"

She was nodding. "I think I know who you mean. Sarat. An old man who seems angry? I remember now. You came with a friend. You were invited for a meal here, and ate nothing. He was angry. You are right." She lowered her voice. "He often gets angry."

"Can I see him? I have to make it right." She rolled up one of her sleeves to show her stick arm. "You see?"

"Oh, yes. I know," she said. "But I am afraid. He does not often talk to strangers. But I will try." Glee left and slipped inside another hut. Frankie heard an angry, old voice, then Glee's gentle voice. Then the angry man's voice again. Glee came back.

"He will not see you. He says you are getting what you deserve."

Frankie stood there in shock. After all this? To be dismissed without a word? "I must see him," she said.

"He won't see you. I asked." Glee looked at Frankie in sympathy. "I am sorry."

"What can I do?"

Glee thought. "Stay with us. Your only chance is somehow to try to reach him. There is nothing I can do. There is nothing anyone can do but him. And," she lowered her voice, "he is a powerful person. We are all a little scared of him."

Frankie nodded. She tried not to look as panicked as she felt. "I have a gift for him," she said.

"Give it to him," Glee said. Then she smiled at Frankie. "Stay with me."

"I don't want to put you in danger," Frankie said.

"You won't. He likes me as well as he likes anyone. Well, that's not quite true. He likes children."

"I will stay with you, then. And I thank you so much for your kindness." Frankie picked up her backpack. She put it in Glee's hut.

When Frankie thought the time was right, she gave the old man the knife she had brought for him. He looked at it. Then he gave her a thin smile. He threw the knife in the dirt and walked back to his hut.

Frankie didn't give up. For the next few days she was as charming as she could be. She laughed and ate everything. She even choked down the curly black thing on the plate that she could not identify. The old man watched her at every meal. He had a small smile on his face. And she was still getting thinner. One night, after dinner, she put her head in her hands in Glee's hut and burst into tears. Glee fluttered around her, patting her. But Frankie had seen the future. She would stay here and get thinner until she died. She could not leave—her only hope was here.

Now Frankie began to change. She drifted from day to day. She didn't smile. She no longer tried to talk to the old man. His hut was just next door. She ate, slept, and tried to make her mind blank.

One day she was sitting in front of Glee's hut when some of the children ran by. They laughed at one another. Something about the flashing smiles touched her. Frankie smiled at them. They smiled back and asked her to play. She now knew enough of their language to answer back. Yes, she would. They played for hours. By the end of the afternoon, Frankie had an idea. She brought out the rest of the high-energy bars she had. Until now, she had forgotten all about them. She gave them to the children. They loved the shiny wrappers. They opened them carefully, saving the foil. Then they tried the bars. They were full of figs and sugar. The children loved them. Frankie laughed. It was the first time she had laughed in weeks. I really am giving up, Frankie thought. Those bars were my food for the trip home. There is no choice now. I will die here. She closed her eyes.

Next to her, she heard shuffling. The old man was there. He looked at her narrowly. Then he called to Glee. She came running. The old man talked to her. Glee looked at Frankie. "He wants me to tell you what he says." Frankie nodded.

"He says he saw you give the food to the children. He says that is what he was waiting for. Some sign that you had a nice spirit in you. You come once and look at us as if we are dirt." Glee said. "These are his words, not mine. He says first you look that way. Then you want something and come back. Then you take, take, take, and never give. Now you give. So he takes the spell off." The old man grunted and nodded at Frankie. His old eyes looked straight into hers. He said exactly five words. Then he walked back to his hut.

"That's it?" asked Frankie to Glee, in shock.

Glee nodded. "He told me I could tell you nothing. It was so hard. But now you will be fine. Not too much longer, and you would have died. That would have been very hard to watch."

Frankie looked at Glee. Frankie was speechless. All along, that old man had wanted something? And it was for her to be *nice?* Frankie felt a little ashamed. She was also angry. To die because you didn't know the right thing to do—what fairness was that? But it was over. Frankie felt a surge of joy. She was sure that she would be all right now. She tried to sort out her feelings. What had she learned? Maybe that the world is a strange place. But it never hurts to be nice.

Think About It

1. Why was Frankie getting thinner and thinner?
2. Why did Sarat put the curse on Frankie?
3. What good qualities did you see in Frankie? What qualities does she have that you did not like?

Before You Read
Here's everything you need to know to be listed as the youngest person ever to eat a telephone booth: a how-to guide for the famous *Guinness Book of Records*.

So You Want to Get Into the *Guinness Book of Records?*

The things people do to get in the *Guinness Book of Records*.

Take the case of Stefan Sigmond. He ate 29 hard-boiled eggs in four minutes just to get into The Book.

And what did Mr. Sigmond get for his trouble? Nothing. Let's hope he had some fun doing those strange things. The *Guinness Book of Records* wanted nothing to do with him.

Today, the more than 40-year-old book of records won't post records for things like stuffing yourself. That ended in 1990. Too dangerous, the editors said. Besides, this is a world in which people are starving. How can we write about a person who ate the most hot dogs when some people can't afford to buy one?

They also tell people to forget daredevil acts. Still, the book lists some strange ones. For example, there is Daniel Goodwin. He used suction cups and metal clips to help him climb 1,454 feet up the Sears Tower in Chicago.

Or there is the case of the U.S. Air Force trying, it seemed, to cook its own men. The Air Force ran experiments in 1960 to see how much they could heat up people—and still keep them alive. The answer? A naked man could stand temperatures of up to 400 degrees. A man wearing clothes could stand temperatures up to 500 degrees. Remember, many people cook steaks at 325 degrees.

So, let's say you have decided you won't try anything as nutty as Stefan Sigmond. How might you get into The Book? First of all, get ready to fail. The editor in charge of letters, Amanda Brooks, gets about 10,000 letters a year. They are all from people who think they have broken a world record. Here is one.

Dear ma'am or sir,

My name is Ethan Whittet, and I am eleven years old.

In October of 1992 I stretched three pieces of bubble gum 31 feet and three inches.

Please let me know if this is a world record, or if you need more information.

You can write to me.

Thank you,
Ethan Whittet

• • •

Ethan may have set a record, but it wasn't a record that The Book would recognize. Even so, some people do succeed. Here is what it takes.

1. You must be able to measure the record that you are making.
2. The act of making a record must be seen by someone else. The person watching you make a record must be able to prove he or she saw it.
3. The record you set must be something that someone besides you cares about. Strange skills and things that happen only once do not make it into The Book.

So, let's say you still want to set a record. Here are some of the records you might try to break.

- Make a very large rice pudding. In 1993, the New York Guild of Chefs made one that weighed 2,146.6 pounds. After it was finished, 2,600 people ate it.
- Do the most sit-ups in 24 hours. Lou Scripa, Jr., has that record. He did 70,715 during a 24 hour period between December 1 and 2 in 1992.
- Talk fast. Steve Woodmore has that record. He spoke 637.4 words in one minute.
- Make a bed. The record for making a bed is 28.8 seconds. The record holder is Wendy Wall.
- Juggle. Anthony Gatto juggled five clubs without dropping any—and he did it for 45 minutes and 2 seconds.

How did the *Guinness Book of Records* begin? Two men were arguing over which kind of bird was fastest. They went to the library. They couldn't find the answer. That got one of the men thinking. There must be arguments like this going on all over the place, he thought. Maybe I should put together a book of records. The man, Hugh Beaver, asked two people to write the book for him.

The result was the *Guinness Book of Records*. It was first published in England in 1955. As soon as it came out, it was the top best-seller in Europe. The next year, the U.S. version of the book came out. In 1995, the book was published in 30 languages.

What kinds of things are in the book? If it's in heaven or earth, or of interest to lots of people, you can probably find it. The book has information about people. You can find out who has the record for the most marriages, and who is the tallest person in the world.

There are records about the world. For example, do you know the noisiest animal in the world? (It is the howler monkey.) How about the hottest temperature ever in the United States? (In Death Valley, California, the temperature once reached 134 degrees.)

You can find out about things that you never thought about before. Who would guess that there really is a man who calls himself Mr. Eat-Everything? Since 1959, he has eaten about two pounds of metal a day. He has eaten 10 bicycles. He has eaten a supermarket cart. (That took four and a half days.) He has eaten a computer. He has eaten seven TV sets. Doctors don't know how he does it. They say, however, that this is not something you should **ever** try at home.

And speaking of records, the *Guinness Book of Records* holds one itself. It is the best-selling copyrighted book in the world. More than 77 million copies have been sold.

Still interested? Then write to this address to find out more. Don't forget to put in a stamped envelope addressed to you.

Facts on File, Inc.
460 Park Avenue South
New York, NY 10016
Attn: *Guinness Book of Records*

Think About It

1. What did Stefan Sigmond do to get into the *Guinness Book of Records*?

2. Why do you think the people who write the book no longer include most records for doing dangerous things?

3. Do you want to get into the *Guinness Book of Records*? Why or why not?

Before You Read

A poor Puerto Rican girl who wasn't expected to go very far made up her mind to go as far as she wanted. This short story is based on the life of Nicholasa Mohr, an artist and writer.

A Voice to Tell Her Story

The Puerto Rican girl sat down as her counselor looked up from the folder she was holding. She had a bright, false smile on her face. "Well, well. And who is this? Nicholasa?"

Nicholasa nodded.

"It's time to choose a high school. Now, I'm sure you won't be going on to college. Right? Let's find you a nice high school where you can learn something useful. Like how to sew." She looked up at Nicholasa. The bright smile was still on the woman's mouth.

Nicholasa opened and closed her mouth. She felt her face turn bright red. "But—but—"

"Oh, come now," the counselor said. "We want you to have something to do when you get out of high school. Right?"

"I don't want to." The words came out quietly. The woman looked up sharply.

"You don't want to what?" Her voice was as sharp as her look.

"I don't want to sew. I want to study art in college."

"That's very nice, I'm sure," the woman said. She had an edge in her voice. "But getting into college is very hard. And the work is very hard, too.

I think you would be much better off here." And she shut the folder. "Good. That's settled." The woman stood up. Nicholasa realized she was expected to stand, too. Her future had been decided.

Well, it hasn't been decided, Nicholasa thought. I will go to college. I don't care what she thinks of me. She thinks Puerto Ricans are only smart enough to sew. It isn't true. I'm going to show her.

She walked home, hugging her books tight to her chest. She was daydreaming. Going away to college. Then a brilliant career. "Hey, you!" The voice was loud and rude. Confused, Nicholasa looked up. Was that voice talking to her?

"Yes, you," the voice said again. Nicholasa turned around. A policeman stood looking at her. His hands were on his hips. He had a look of disgust on his face. "I'm looking for one of you people. A Juan Ricardo. You know him?"

Nicholasa shook her head.

"You must. He's one of you," the policeman said. "Don't lie to me. You look like that girl he hangs out with. Where is he?"

"I don't know him," she said.

"Eh, just get lost," the policeman said with disgust. He dismissed her with his hand. Then he walked away.

Nicholasa looked down. Even though she had done nothing, the policeman had made her feel dirty and small. She sighed as she walked up the three floors to her family's apartment. What a day.

Nicholasa's family lived in the Bronx, a part of New York City. Her parents had moved there from Puerto Rico in the 1930s. It was often noisy on the streets.

Inside the tiny apartment, her brothers were running around. The appartment seemed even smaller than usual.

Nicholasa looked at the shabby rooms. She sighed. When she felt like this, there was only one escape.

When she had been a small girl, her mother had given her some scrap paper and a few crayons. She drew pictures that showed a world of beauty. If the world around her was sometimes painful, at least the world in her mind was not.

Nicholasa's mother had looked at the drawings she made and clasped her hands together. "Ah, my little daughter! You are special. You have these wonderful talents. You must study. You must use these talents."

The words came back to Nicholasa as she drew. As always, the memory of those words made her sad. Nicholasa's mother had died. Now there was no one to look at her pictures with admiring eyes. No one to say she was special. But still, Nicholasa thought, she would be an artist when she grew up. She would do it no matter what anyone said.

Nicholasa's aunt came to take her mother's place. The aunt was distant. She did not understand her niece's love of beauty. The aunt had no use for art. And no use for a girl she considered lazy for wanting to lie around drawing.

All six of Nicholasa's brothers were nice, but they thought of her as only a girl. In some ways, her family thought the same way about her as the counselor. She should grow up. She should marry a nice Puerto Rican man. She should stay home and raise the children. She should forget about doing anything else like being an artist. She respected women who stayed home and worked hard to care for their families. But Nicholasa wanted to draw.

Nicholasa had found comfort in her art before. Now it was her life. The colors on the page helped her remember her mother. She could forget the problems at school.

She could forget the names she was called on the street. She could forget the people who thought she should dream of growing up to be a good wife and mother. She could lose herself in the world of color and shape and line.

As she drew that night, she thought more about the counselor's words. And she decided not to give in to the pressure. She would go to a high school that she chose, one with a good art program.

Nicholasa struggled until she got what she wanted. She was able to get into a high school of fashion and design. At least there she could draw. While she was there, Nicholasa never lost sight of her dream. After she graduated, she began to study at the Art Students League in New York.

It wasn't easy. Nicholasa worked as a waitress and as a translator. She worked in an office. She also paid for school and saved a little money. Someday, she dreamed, she would travel to Europe. She would visit Paris and Rome. She would study the art of the masters.

Finally, she had saved enough money to go to Europe. She sat planning the trip with a friend.

"In the past few weeks, I've been studying the muralists in Mexico. Have you seen their work? It speaks to me. It is powerful in a way that touches me deep inside. These are artists with something to say. They use bold colors. The lines they make are strong. Next to them, these French painters seem—well, they seem weak."

Amy studied her. "You want to go to Mexico instead of Europe? Are you crazy?"

"I'm not crazy. I know what I want. I want to go to Mexico. It's just that when you have a dream for years, and then you find out it was the wrong dream—" She paused. "I guess it's just confusing."

Amy was shaking her head. "Well, I'm not confused. I wouldn't miss going to Europe for anything." She looked at Nicholasa. "But you've always been different. Well," she said, standing up, "I can see where this is going. Let me know when you get back. I want to find out what you think about Mexico then."

Mexico was more exciting than Nicholasa had ever imagined. The art was even stronger up close. The faces in the murals had the strength of a people. They were powerful. Nicholasa studied the art carefully.

When she came back to New York, she began studying again. In school, she met a special man, Irwin Mohr. They married and had two sons. But Nicholasa was not the mother her family expected. She still painted. Her work was colorful and bold. You could see the effect of her time in Mexico in her painting. But the art was also filled with symbols of New York. You could read the stories of life in the streets. There were numbers, words, and faces in the pictures. It was her view of New York.

Nicholasa's art began to sell. She worked hard. She also taught art. She did some illustrations for book covers. Then a publisher who liked her work called her to talk.

"I've got an idea," he said. "What about doing some writing?"

"Me?" she asked. "I don't write."

"Well, you ought to think about it," he told her.

She hung up thoughtfully. Over the next few days, she considered the idea. She thought about her life growing up in New York. She had read great stories—but they had always been about children who were not Puerto Rican. She had never read a story about a Puerto Rican girl. She also realized that she'll never read about

people like her brothers, parents, or neighbors. Puerto Ricans needed to be able to read about themselves, she thought. People who were not Puerto Rican needed to find out what it felt like to be called "you people." They needed to see how unfairly Puerto Ricans are treated.

Nicholasa made up her mind. Why not give it a try? She called up the publisher. She agreed to write 50 pages of short stories. They would be about growing up as a Puerto Rican in New York City.

She wrote the stories and turned them in. The publisher said the stories weren't good enough. The rejection was just a signal for Nicholasa to try harder. When another publisher called her to draw a book cover, she brought in her stories instead.

Three weeks later, Nicholasa picked up the mail. She noticed a letter from the publisher. She opened it. Inside was a contract for a book. The publisher had liked what he read. He wanted her to write a novel based on her stories.

Nicholasa sat down to write. It was like her first days of crayons and paper at home. The words flew from her pen. She wrote of being called "you people" by policemen. She wrote of the pain of being called names by classmates. She had her main character, Nilda, going off to camp. While she was at camp, the other children made fun of her for not having a real suitcase. The pain was real. It was based on her life as a child. And it showed exactly what Nicholasa wanted. It showed what life was like for a poor Puerto Rican girl with big dreams in New York City.

Unsure of her work, but still proud, Nicholasa put the pages into an envelope. Then she mailed it to the publisher. She didn't have to wait long for a response.

"Nicholasa? I've read it. It's great. You've written a winner. Just wait and see."

The publisher was right. The book was an instant success. "A book by which others may be judged," wrote one critic. She won awards for her writing. The book, *Nilda,* was named one of the best books of the year. Nicholasa also won awards for the book cover, which she had painted.

Since then, the girl who was supposed to grow up to get a job sewing has written many more books. She has also won many more awards.

Nicholasa Mohr still paints and writes. She has come to love writing. "I can draw pictures with words," she says. And for a young Puerto Rican girl just discovering *Nilda,* it is a welcome picture. Reading the book is knowing that you are not alone. It is knowing that others have dealt with hard times, and gotten through them. It is finding a voice that tells your story.

"There is a crying need for what I had to say as a Puerto Rican," Nicholasa says. She may have grown up often feeling alone. She has made sure that those who follow her writings and art do not have to feel that way.

Note: Nicholasa Mohr has written many books for young people. They reflect her life. If you are interested in Nicholasa Mohr and want to read one of her books, try her first novel, Nilda. *It is the story of a young Puerto Rican girl in New York City.*

Think About It

1. Why did Nicholasa go to Mexico instead of Europe to study art?
2. Why did Nicholasa Mohr decide to try writing?
3. What subject would you use if you were writing a story or painting a picture? Why?

Before You Read
Many Native Americans have gone on quests for visions. In these stories, meet a boy who saw the stars dance, a chief who got his power from a mouse, and others.

Visions on the Plains

12 Junction
Daw, Kansas

June 12, 1850

Dear Mr. Jackson,

I hope this letter reaches you. I heard from a friend of your interest in my work. I am happy to share my work. I do not have any items for your museum. However, I do have information. I am writing this letter to tell you what I know about the quest for visions among the Native Americans. I hear that is one of your interests. I have a deep interest in the lives of the Native Americans that I have met. This is why I have studied vision quests. For forty years, I have run trading posts here. I am deeply honored to be asked to share what I know.

First, I should tell you that I write about the Plains Native Americans. There are many tribes in this group. They have different customs. Many tribes are enemies of other Plains tribes. I tell you this because I often hear about "the Indians," as if they were one group. Believe me, sir, they are not. There are some things these tribes have in common. But they are also different in many other important ways.

I will tell you some stories about a search for a vision. The Native Americans I know seek visions to tell them what to do about a problem or to gain wisdom. They also seek visions to gain the blessing of a spirit.

The Plains Indians I know are very spiritual. Their god or gods are the spirit of the earth itself. It is in these spirits the Indians seek the truth. The following stories were told to me by a Chief of the Hidatsa tribe.

The Hidatsa Boy

In the Hidatsa tribe, up north, a boy was sent away by his father to get the blessing of a spirit. The son, Tall Corn, was seven when he was sent. The father believed his son needed this blessing. The son seemed troubled. Sending him out to seek a vision was the way to calm his spirit. It would show him his path in life.

Tall Corn looked like his father. Like him, he had a proud way. He told me that the vision he was sent to find did change his life.

He was sent to the mountains in early spring. He was told to fast for three days and pray to the spirits. Tall Corn told me that he was frightened when he left. He was only seven, of course.

Tall Corn followed a well-known path up to the mountains. The Hidatsa are a tribe that lives to the far north. It was still cold when Tall Corn left. He described walking up a path still wet from the melting snow. After hours of walking, he saw a break in the path to his right. He headed for the break. He found himself in a clearing. He was on a ledge. Far below, he could see the smoke from the fires of his village.

For three days, he stayed on the ledge. He only got up to drink water from a stream nearby. He was hungry, of course. But after the second day, he said, the hunger changed to a dull ache. On the third night, he said, he was staring at the stars when something happened.

First, I should explain about the stars. On a mountain like the one Tall Corn was on, the stars are so bright, and there are so many of them. They fill up the world at night.

The stars, Tall Corn said, began to move. They swirled in the darkness as he watched. They changed places in the sky. Finally, they placed themselves in a pattern and stayed there, he said. The stars formed a picture of a field of corn. It was just planted. But around the corn was snow.

Tall Corn stared at the stars, puzzled. What did this mean? He was quite sure that there was a reason for this picture. For hours he stared. The picture stayed the same. Still, it was corn, early corn, with snow.

Suddenly, Tall Corn said he understood. This year, the corn had to be planted early. Otherwise, the harvest would be poor. As soon as he understood this, he said, the stars changed again. They formed a glowing ball in the center of the sky. Tall Corn said he then knew he had understood.

He slept on the ledge that night, then came down to his village the next morning. His father told me that Tall Corn entered the village with a new walk. He was confident, the chief said. He had lost his troubled look.

Tall Corn told his father what had happened. Among the Hidatsa, visions like Tall Corn's are taken seriously. The chief ordered the village to begin planting early that year.

The chief told me that when someone went off to receive a vision about themselves, they would learn something very different. But for Tall Corn, the vision spoke to him and to his tribe. Tall Corn's vision had made him feel his worth to the village. It had given him an importance. Later that year, when the corn was safely planted and growing, a terrible drought came. No rain fell for a month. But because the corn had been planted early, it did not die.

The Eagle Who Befriended a Crow

This story was told to me by a Crow Native American who always carried a symbol of an eagle. I asked him why. He told me this story about his vision quest.

The man's name was One-Who-Listens and he went to the woods alone to seek a vision because his people had been attacked many times by another tribe. He wanted to know what to do. So he went on a vision quest. For four days he didn't eat. He listened to the water in streams. He heard the wind in the trees. And he waited and hoped for a vision.

On the fourth day, he said, it began to storm. The fourth day, by the way, is very important in Crow traditions. It is a mystical number. One-Who-Listens stood up in the rain and opened his mouth to drink the water. He also opened his eyes, he said, to feel the water fall on him. At that moment, he saw lightning and heard a clap of thunder right over him. The sound filled the world, One-Who-Listens said. And as he watched, the lightning became an eagle. The eagle streaked across the sky. Then the eagle came to a tree and landed on a branch near One-Who-Listens. The man said he knew instantly what the eagle meant. He was a protector. He would make sure the tribe was safe from its enemies.

One-Who-Listens promised to honor the eagle to thank the bird. For that reason, he always wore the symbol of the eagle. Then, from a tiny pouch, One-Who-Listens pulled out an eagle feather. It was a feather from the eagle, he said. It was the most important thing he owned.

The Child Who Was Cured by Sage

This story was told to me by a member of the Arapaho tribe. A man named Water Seeker, told me he went to find a vision when his young child was ill.

His child was a five-year old girl and the delight of her father's life. She was, he told me proudly, a favorite among his people. She was beautiful, with bright eyes and a wide smile. She was known as the child who laughed. She was also his only child. Her mother had died giving birth to her.

One day, the child became ill. She no longer laughed, or even talked. She refused to eat. At night, she moaned.

Water Seeker was worried. The medicine man of the tribe could not cure her. Day by day, Water Seeker watched as his beloved child faded before his eyes.

Finally, he decided that he must seek a vision to cure her. He went to a sacred place in the mountain. For four days, he prayed. It was not hard, he said. He would have done it for months if he had thought it would help his daughter.

Like One-Who-Listens, on the fourth day, he had a vision. His dead wife came to him, he said. She told him to go to another mountain, where wild sage grew. He was to gather the sage and rub it on the child's forehead for a week. He was also to burn the sage in a fire where the child could breathe the smoke.

Water Seeker quickly went to the other mountain, got the sage, and returned to his village. There, his daughter was sicker than before, he said. For a week, he rubbed sage on her forehead. He also burned sage in the fire. For the first few days, the child stayed the same.

On the sixth day, he said, she opened her eyes. She asked to eat. After that, she recovered from her illness.

The Boy Who Saved a Mouse

This story comes from the Pawnee tribe. It was told to me by a very old man who said it happened to him when he was a small child. This man was a great chief.

His people thought he had the power of the spirit in him because of the story he told me.

Even as a young boy, the chief said, he had believed in spirits. He also believed that he had a special purpose in life. When he was six, he asked to seek a vision.

His parents thought that he was too young. He could not go without food for days, as was needed for a vision quest.

However, the boy thought differently. He left home early one morning, telling only his sister of his plans. He warned her not to tell their parents until he was far away.

The boy went to a special place he knew. He stayed there, for three days. He didn't eat and prayed.

During these days, the chief said, he became interested in a group of field mice that had a nest near where he sat. As he stayed there motionless, day after day, the mice began to treat him as if he were just another part of the landscape. They ran around him. He watched them, amused at their comings and goings. Then one of the mice came too close to a hole in the ground. The hole might have been dug as a trap by a larger animal, the chief said. He did not know. The mouse fell in the hole. However, once in the hole, the boy heard its tiny cries. It seemed to the boy that the mouse was asking for help.

The boy reached down and scooped up the mouse. Then he put it on the ground. The chief said the mouse turned and looked at the boy. The look was a knowing one. Without saying anything, the mouse told the boy that he would be rewarded for his kindness. The boy now had power.

It was as clear what he had heard, the chief said. The boy realized that this was the answer to his vision quest. He had his vision. He also had a power that the mouse had granted him, honesty.

When he came back, he said, he felt different. The man who was then chief of the tribe took him in as his son. From then, it was understood that the boy would grow up to be a chief himself. He had a power to share with his tribe. Indeed, the chief was known as a man of honesty. He was respected by his tribe for his wisdom. He was also respected by other tribes as well, who saw him as a man to trust.

...As a modern man, I have my doubts about these stories. What are we to think about a child becoming well from sage smoke? Who can know what causes a cure? Perhaps the child felt the love of her father and got better.

Or think of the chief who helped the mouse. Perhaps he was meant to be a chief from his youth.

I do not know if these visions are real. I only know the Native Americans I talked to believe they were real. Perhaps all anyone needs is a belief in themself.

I am happy to be of help to you in your work. As your plans for your museum progress, please keep me informed. I look forward to your visit here in April.

Sincerely,
Justin Cade

Think About It

1. Why did Justin Cade write this letter?
2. How did helping the mouse change the life of the Pawnee boy?
3. What is Justin Cade's view of the stories he was told? Do you think he believes them, or not?

Before You Read
Have you ever wondered why people do something as risky as climbing a dangerous mountain? Can you think of something risky that you'd like to do when you're an adult?

The Call of Everest

J.N Fox

The stone and ice of the mountain call.
Most climbers settle
for telling tales of safer peaks
and shorter treks.
But those who answer
the call of Everest
learn only of extremes
and nothing in between:
agony, peril, life and death.

Think About It

1. Why do you think most mountain climbers settle for "safer peaks and shorter treks"?

2. What do you think makes people want to climb a dangerous mountain like Mount Everest?

3. If you could meet a mountain climber, what questions would you ask him/her?

Before You Read
An alarming disease was spreading in Connecticut, and no one knew why. In this true story, medical detectives solve the mystery.

The Disease Hunter

Polly Murray was worried. The trouble had begun when one of her children became sick. Her child had a strange rash. She also had headaches that would not go away. Then she got stiff knees.

Polly's husband then became sick. Before long, two of her children, and her husband, were on crutches. Whatever they had, it hurt. And nobody knew what to do about it.

Polly talked to friends. "You know, my child has the same thing," one told her. Then she found out about another, and another.

Something was making people near Lyme, Connecticut, very sick.

At Yale University, Allen Steere got a call about the strange disease. The scientist was studying arthritis. Arthritis is a disease in which people's joints, such as their knees, get stiff. That was what the Murray family seemed to have. Steere went looking. What he found was a surprising number of people in Connecticut with swollen, stiff knees. They also had other stiff joints. They seemed to have the same sickness that was affecting the Murray family.

Allen Steere kept finding more and more sick people. He was puzzled. Arthritis wasn't something you could catch. You couldn't get it from someone else like the measles. And yet all these people seemed to have arthritis. Something else was very strange. Children rarely get arthritis of any kind.

The more Dr. Steere looked in the countryside, the more cases he found. In some places, one out of every ten children seemed to have the strange arthritis. "I was astonished," he told the *National Geographic* magazine. "It seemed almost certain we were looking at a new disease."

Steere had begun a year-long search to solve the mystery.

He began to gather information. He asked the sick people many questions. "Where have you been? What did you notice before you got sick? Where were you just before you got sick?"

He put dots on the map of where all the sick people lived. Then Steere stared at the map. Was there a pattern to where the cases turned up? Could the people who got sick be spreading the disease to each other? Or was something else causing it?

In Lyme, Connecticut, there were 39 children and 12 adults with the mystery disease. Steere put more dots on the map for each person. He stared at the dots. He saw something. All the people who got sick lived in places where there were many trees.

Trees. Trees. Okay–that was a clue. What else did these cases have in common? Steere knew that most of the people first got sick in summer or early fall. What happens in the woods in summer and early fall?

Suddenly he had an idea, insects. Steere thought about the trees. He thought about how many insects there were in the area in the summer. That could be it, he thought.

Steere looked over his notes again. There were several patients who said that just before they had become sick, they noticed a strange rash. It looked like a round red circle with a dot in the middle, just like a bull's-eye.

Then, another doctor told Steere about a rash he had heard about in a nearby Connecticut town. The rash, the doctor said, sounded like a rash in Europe. The rash is called ECM.

Steere looked up ECM. Patients with ECM get a rash. They get some of the other symptoms, too. Some think the disease is caused by a sheep tick. A tick. That would fit, Steere thought. It's good tick country in those Connecticut woods.

Then, in 1977, a patient brought Steere the tick that had bitten him. It was a tick that was very common in the wooded areas where people had been getting sick. Soon, the patient had the bull's-eye rash.

Steere felt he was getting closer to identifying the new disease. The next step was to find more of the ticks. Researchers got to work. They pulled cloths through the bushes around the city of Lyme to collect ticks. They found plenty. They also found that the ticks were almost the same type as the sheep ticks in Europe. But no one had ever seen this particular tick before.

In 1979, a scientist named Andrew Spielman told the world that the tick was a new species called *Ixodes dammini.* A species is a plant or animal that is different than any other type.

Dr. Spielman found that the new tick lives for two years. In late summer, the larvae, or eggs, hatch on an animal. Usually that is a white-footed mouse. It sucks the animal's blood as food. In the spring, the tick larva grows again and has another meal of blood.

Sometimes it sucks blood from a person. By the fall, the adult tick has its last meal of blood. This meal is usually blood sucked from a white-tailed deer. The adult tick is only the size of a large speck of dust.

Two years after the tick was first found, scientists learned something important. Dr. Willy Burgdorfer proved that a bacteria in the tick caused the strange disease. The disease is now named Lyme disease because it was first noticed in Lyme, Connecticut.

What happens, exactly? Other scientists found that the mice that the ticks feed on also often have the bacteria. When the ticks bite the mice, they get the bacteria. Then, the ticks bite another animal. When the tick bites, it passes the bacteria to the animal or person it bites. Then the person develops the disease.

Still other scientists found that the bacteria had been around the East Coast in ticks since the 1940s. Back then, though, few, if any, people were getting sick. What happened?

Since the 1940s, the number of ticks has grown. There are many more forests now. The forests that were cut back then have been allowed to grow back. Also, the number of deer has risen. That meant that there was good eating for the *I. dammini* tick.

Finding the answer to this puzzle has not stopped Lyme disease. Today, it is still a big problem. Many thousands of people get the disease every year. Most of these people are on the East Coast. That is where most of the ticks live.

Health experts tell people who live near woods or fields in the East to be careful. They tell people to wear long pants, and tuck their pants into their shoes. They tell them to wear long-sleeved shirts, and hats. Still, in the summer many people want to feel the sun on their arms and legs.

It is hard to tell children, who love to play outside in the summer, to wear long pants.

There is still no way to keep people from getting the disease. But finding out what it is, and what causes it, has made a big difference in many people's lives. People understand how to prevent it now. They know to look for a bull's-eye rash. They know that if they live on the East Coast and feel sick, Lyme disease could be the reason.

Best of all, there are ways to treat Lyme disease, now that doctors know what it is. If patients are treated just after they get sick, they will be cured. A drug called tetracycline kills the bacteria. But if people are not treated soon after they get sick, they can have bad problems. They may develop arthritis that lasts for years. This arthritis makes their joints swell and hurt. The bacteria may also attack the heart and brain. Even at this stage, though, large doses of penicillin can still cure the disease.

Before the detective work of Allen Steere and others, people like Polly Murray had a reason to be scared of the disease. With hard work and luck, scientists solved the mystery. When people in the East see that bull's-eye rash now, they may be afraid. But they should also know that they can be cured.

Think About It

1. What are the symptoms of Lyme disease?
2. Why have there been more cases of Lyme disease since the 1940s?
3. How can you avoid getting Lyme disease?

Before You Read

Three dangerous men are brought together by a search for gold. Who will double-cross whom? And why?

Rule of Gold

The campfire lit the faces of three men. They were not pretty faces. They were not faces that would be at home with fine china and soft fluffy pillows. These were hard men.

Three men sat around the fire. There was Marcus Jones. He was a drifter who had come out as soon as he heard the news. Next to him sat Spider Malone. Spider kept glancing quickly to his right and left. His eyes were narrow. It was as if he thought that any moment, someone would try to get the best of him. The third man was a talker. Mud Graves got his name from liking to talk. One day, a fellow got tired of listening to him and threw mud at Graves. Mud never learned his lesson. He was the one talking now.

"So, the way I see it, we head out over there. That's close to where the Finley brothers got their strike. We'll just go up higher than they did on the mountain." He chuckled. "Yeah, that's the thing. Head up above the creek. Sure strike. We'll be rich before you know it, rich and then—"

"Aw, shut up." That was Marcus. "We're tired of listening to you. Just shut your trap."

"Well, now, that's a fine thing. Who are you to tell me what to do? Besides, we need a plan, don't we?"

"Just shut up. I'm thinking," Marcus growled. The three men sat in silence for a moment. Marcus had a stick in his hand, drawing in the dirt. "Are we together or are we apart? There's no reason to be together unless we think so. We don't really know each other." He looked at Mud. For once, Mud stayed quiet.

The Colorado night grew colder. A coyote howled in the distance. Mud shivered. "I'm with you," he muttered.

"Me too," said Spider.

Marcus looked around. "Then we need some rules. And a plan. Here's the first rule. All for one, and one for all. Agreed?"

The other two nodded.

"Like I said. We don't know each other," Marcus said. "But we're all here for the same thing, gold. And if we stick together, we'll be better off." The other two nodded again.

"Fine, then. I got another idea," he said. Then he scowled at Mud.

"So what's your plan?" Spider said. He spoke quickly, in a jerky voice. His eyes were jerky, too.

"The plan is this. We go out together. Then we split up. Anyone finds any gold, he gives a shout. Or, if he's too far away, we meet back here for dinner every day. Got it?"

"Sounds good," Mud said. "We can start in the morning."

Morning came quickly. While the sky was still streaked red, the men were sipping coffee at the fire. Mud pointed with his cup. "I'm heading over there. He saw some rock that looked good. See you at dinner." And he left. The other two weren't far behind.

Over a plate of beans and bacon that night, they traded news."Looked good, but nah," said Mud.

"Same here," Spider said. He looked down at his plate. Marcus grunted.

It was the same story for about a week. No gold.

Then another week. Then a month. Now the differences between the men became clear. Mud was sad. He sighed all the time. He frowned. He fidgeted. "Thought we'd have something by now," he said often. Too often for the other two.

Marcus seemed to get more set on finding the gold. He left earlier. He worked longer. He had a hard set to his face. He had stopped being a drifter. He had one thought on his mind. That was finding gold.

Spider was the hardest to read. He worked as much as the others, but his eyes darted around. He asked questions about what the other men had found. The questions made the others believe Spider didn't trust them. They had more than one fight with Spider.

They slowly drifted into a way of life. Each day they got up, ate their breakfast, then walked off for a day of looking. They came home, ate, talked for a while, and went to sleep.

Then Marcus got strange. He wouldn't tell the others where he was headed. He talked in single words. Something was going on. This went on for a week or so.

"Come on," Spider said one night over another plate of beans. "You been acting edgy for a week. What gives?"

"Nothing. Nothing," Marcus muttered. He would say nothing more. Spider looked at him. His eyes were narrowed. Mud didn't say anything either. He kept his eyes on his food as he ate. Then he rolled over and went to sleep.

The next day, Spider waited until Marcus and Mud had left. He stayed around the fire. Took a while to sharpen his knife. Wiped his dishes extra well. Then he took off after Marcus.

He moved softly. He stepped lightly. He stayed just out of Marcus's sight. That wasn't easy. Marcus was looking around the whole time. Like he expected to be followed. Spider grinned to himself. He had a feeling he knew what Marcus was up to. And he wasn't going to get away with it.

Finally, Marcus stopped. He looked carefully around him. Satisfied, he climbed down to a stream. He pulled out a pan from his shirt and began panning for gold. "Son of a gun," Spider thought. "He's panning. We've all been looking in the hills, and he's in the stream. And finding something, I'd bet."

Spider spent the morning watching. Marcus found a couple of nuggets. Put them in his pocket. Kept going. Finally, Marcus stopped for lunch.

Spider stepped out. He was grinning. "So, thief. How you doing?"

"Who are you calling a thief?" Marcus said hotly. His mouth was full.

"You rotten pig. Did you forget our deal?"

"I forgot nothing. But I started thinking about it, Marcus replied. "Why should I let you have the benefit of my hard work? Who has been breaking his back here? We ain't got no deal. Nothing that's legal."

"I'll show you legal," said Spider. Then he pulled out a gun.

"You're going to shoot me?" Marcus said. Spider could tell from his voice that Marcus didn't really know what he'd do.

"Maybe," he said softly. "Maybe not. You had any more thoughts about our agreement?"

"Yeah. Yeah. Sure. You can have your share. Put away the gun."

Spider put away the gun. "OK, let's talk. Actually, now that I think about it, maybe we don't need a deal— with that idiot, Mud. He can go his way. I'll stick with you. What do you say? You can't do this all by yourself, anyway."

Marcus looked at him. "I could. But I'll let you in. But that Mud—he's out." The other man nodded in agreement.

It wasn't hard to fool Mud. The man was so busy talking he didn't pay any attention to what was happening. Every day, Marcus would leave. Then, a few minutes later, Spider would leave. He'd take a different way. They'd meet up by the stream. Then they'd begin panning.

By the end of the month, Marcus and Spider could hardly contain their excitement. They laughed for hours at stupid jokes. They hummed. Somehow, Mud was still without a clue.

"Hey, you guys—had any luck?" he would ask once in a while. He barely waited for them to try to put on gloomy faces before talking more. "Me neither. Too bad, huh?" he would say. Then he'd talk more, whatever came to him.

One day, Marcus and Spider were sure the game was up. They were hooting over a large nugget Spider had found. Then they heard Mud's voice. "Anyone there? Anyone there?"

Quickly, they grabbed their stuff. They hid behind bushes. After a minute, Mud left.

"What you think?" Mud said to himself. "You think

they're here. Naw. They wouldn't be. Musta just thought I heard something. I know. Musta been the stream down there I bet I . . . " Mud's voice trailed off. He was still talking to himself as he walked away.

Spider and Marcus waited a second. Then they broke into hoots of laughter. "If he had eyes in his head," Spider gasped. He was still laughing. He wiped his eyes.

Marcus finished his sentence. "We'd be in big trouble."

Spider giggled. He added, "No chance."

Then, about a week later, Marcus slipped in the stream. He gashed his leg. It was bad. Blood ran in the water. It fanned out red. Then it disappeared. Spider watched the blood. Then he saw Marcus's face. He realized Marcus must be in real pain.

Marcus was holding his leg. His eyes were squeezed shut. His mouth was open. "Okay, Okay, steady, pal," Spider said nervously. "It's all right, pal."

Spider grabbed his shirt and ripped a piece from the bottom. He tied up the leg. Then he put Marcus's arm around his shoulder. They limped to camp.

Mud was already there. He looked up when Spider and Marcus dragged into camp. Mud's eyes got wide.

"What happened? What happened? Marcus get hurt? Is he all right? What did you do? Do you need help?" The words flowed on. Neither of the men paid attention. Marcus was groaning. Spider was rubbing his shoulder. Mud hovered around. "Do you want to go to town? Can I get you a cloth? What do you need? You should really be careful out here. That could get infected."

Finally, Marcus roared, "Will you shut up?"

Mud shut up.

Marcus spent a few days at camp, recovering.

The first day after the accident, when Spider left, Marcus gave him a warning look. Spider had been working with Marcus long enough to know what that look meant. Don't even think about keeping a nugget secret. Then Marcus closed his eyes in pain.

The next week, Marcus and Spider were back at work. After a morning of hard work, they quit to take a cool float in the river.

"Think this place is about played out," Spider said, his feet wiggling above the water.

"What you want to do next?" Marcus asked.

"Find a new place. Further on, " Spider said.

"New camp," Marcus said.

"What about Mud?" Spider asked.

"What about him?" Marcus grunted back.

"Well, he ain't exactly easy on the ears. I'm getting tired of him. Talk, talk, talk, that's all he does. Don't it get to you?"

"Nah," Marcus said.

"What? You feeling guilty or something? We don't need him. And I'm tired of him. What do you say we quit him?"

Marcus scratched his neck. "I don't know. Maybe I am feeling guilty. He seems like such a nice kid, somehow. Like his feelings might be hurt if we ditched him."

"You're the one always yelling at him."

"I don't know. He might feel bad if we ditched him."

On the bank, they heard a muffled laugh. Then a voice. "Not hardly," the voice said. Marcus and Spider looked up at the top of the bank. Mud was standing there. In his hand was their clothes. Then Marcus and Spider saw something else in his hands. Their eyes widened. Mud was holding their gold.

"Why, you—" Spider sputtered.

"Yeah?" Mud said cooly. He was way up the side of the bank. Mud was standing next to his horse. There was no way they could catch him. And Mud had their clothes.

"Poor Mud, huh? You idiots. You really think you were so clever? It took me about five minutes to figure out what you were doing. And that you didn't want me to have any part of it. So much for trust. Well, I decided there was no reason for me to have any, either. I also decided there was no reason for me to work. You're doing it all for me. So I just watched you. Watched you work. Watched where you put every nugget. And here they are." He dangled the bulging bag.

Spider tried to think of what he could do to get the bag back. Mud grinned at them. "In the future, boys, think twice before you double-cross someone. And think twice before you underestimate him, either." Mud got on his horse. Then he grinned at them again. "Guess I'll be leaving you in peace now," he said. And he rode away.

The two men in the creek watched as the dust settled. There was silence. Marcus cleared his throat. "Somehow," he said, "I don't feel much like talking. Know what I mean?"

Spider could only nod.

Think About It

1. What rule did the men set before they went off searching for gold?
2. How did Spider realize Marcus had found gold?
3. If you had to choose one of the three characters to depend on, which would it be? Why?

Before You Read

Ponce de Leon sailed with Columbus on his second voyage to America. Later, when he was governor of Puerto Rico, the Spanish king gave Ponce de Leon money to explore. A sailor's journal tells the story of this quest for the fountain of youth.

Fountain of Youth

January 29, 1513—The ship is nearly ready to sail. She is called the *Santa Maria de la Consolación*. We are on a quest for land and gold. Ponce de Leon speaks of something else with great excitement. He has heard of a fountain of youth. Drink at this spring, the natives told him, and you will be young forever. Ponce de Leon is sure we will find this water. Several of us think he is crazy. But what can we do? We are sailors and he is the leader.

February 17, 1513—We have sailed up the river in Puerto Rico and collected food along the way. We have corn and fruit, oil, and vinegar. We have pickled pork. Setting out on a voyage like this makes us all nervous. Ponce de Leon does not know what lies beyond the safety of this island. He only has a lust for gold. And he has his thirst for the water of youth. I heard him talking to Juan Bono de Quejo. He is captain of our small boat. "Juan," he said, "think of it. It is the answer to every man's question. When he finds himself staring at the end of life. Imagine if a drink from the fountain of youth could bring back youth." Then Ponce de Leon touched his skin. Ponce de Leon is 50 now.

He must feel his age creeping upon him. Juan Bono de Quejo just grunted. I could tell he thought Ponce de Leon's quest was silly, but he did not say so.

April 1, 1513—It has been a bad spell. The wind is cold, and rocks the ships. The rain beats on us. It has beaten on us for three days. The sea rolls, and the wind shrieks. We are frightened. Now we are heading north, beyond what is known. Most everyone is scared. Who knows what is beyond this black storm? I am sick at heart.

April 2, 1513—Today, the wind and blackness have cleared some. From above, from the lookout, came a shout. He has sighted land. He pointed west, and when the clouds cleared, we could see a long, low land. It stretched across the horizon. Ponce de Leon was on our ship today. I could see his face. It was the face of a man who thinks he has seen something grand. For him, it probably was. He can rule whatever islands we find here. And if we find the fountain of youth, he gets that, too. We found land at dark today. I cannot see much of the land. It looks to be as rich as other lands we know in this wild place, however.

April 3, 1513—Ponce de Leon and I and several others took a small boat to shore this morning. I was right about the richness of this land. We saw beautiful purple flowers and the trees towering over our heads. Ponce de Leon's eyes were alight. He was sure that this was the place he would find his fountain of youth. We got out of the boat. The sand was white and soft. We planted the flag of Spain. It is always a proud sight. The flag flies in the wind and shows that God has granted Spain this land. Ponce de Leon breathed in the smell of all the green.

Then he declared that this island would be called Pascua Florida. And so it is.

April 4, 1513—We explored this island today. And it may not be an island. There is no sense that this land before us ends. Ponce de Leon is excited. He led us into the green woods. We looked for signs of people. The people would be the only ones to lead us to the fountain of youth, of course. There was no one. We marched on, but there were no signs of any human beings. We got back to our camp on shore, made a fire, and watched the ship at sea as we ate. There were some fruits and berries that looked worth eating. I would not be the first to test them, though. We cooked and ate our food from the ship.

April 8, 1513—We set sail again today. There was no luck on the shore. We traveled quite a bit, and found nothing. We are now sailing south, and still see no sign of this island ending. We were forced ashore, though. The current is so strong here that one of our ships was swept to sea. We anchored. Then, from the shore, we saw Indians waving to us. We rowed toward shore. The welcome was no welcome at all. As we reached the shore, a hail of arrows met us. Quickly, we returned to the ship. Ponce de Leon was angry. "I am sure that those Indians are keeping us away because of the waters," he said. "They are protecting their waters. Well, they cannot stand the power of Spain." They may not have been able to fight Spain. However, with our few ships, we had to sail on.

April 11, 1513—We have had little luck getting ashore. We brought a stone cross ashore to claim the land for God, and were driven away by the Indians.

April 13, 1513—Today, we came close to finding the fountain Ponce de Leon seeks so desperately. Here, in this great bay, the Indians were friendly. We came ashore. In the rocks were springs bubbling from the ground. Ponce de Leon's eyes gleamed. He tried to explain what he sought. They did not understand. Before a minute had passed, he was on his hands and knees, drinking from the spring. Nothing happened, however. He inspected his face, his hands. Still the face and hands of a 50-year-old man. This is no fountain of youth.

May 1, 1513—We have been sailing around islands that match any in beauty. We gasp at the number of birds, and fish, and seals. The fish are of many colors. They dart blue and gold under the waves. It is a marvel.

May 18, 1513—We are retracing our way down the west coast. Ponce de Leon seems more driven than ever with his search. We do not tell him, but we think he may be mad. He searches for something that no man should find, even if it exists.

May 23, 1513—Today began well. We anchored last night at a fine bay. This morning, an Indian who spoke our language came out in a boat. He told us his chief had much gold to trade. Ponce de Leon, his hunger for gold almost as great as his hunger for that water, nodded eagerly. We set ashore in several boats, loaded with goods to trade. We were just ashore when suddenly, the Indians attacked. Twenty canoes full of Indians began shooting arrows. The fight was terrible. We had few guns. Several of our men were hurt.

May 24, 1513—That fool, Ponce de Leon, lets his lust for gold get in the way of sense. "It was a misunderstanding," he said, and sent us back today to trade. This time, we had guns. It was not enough.

This day, there were 80 canoes, each with fighting men set on killing us. Even Ponce de Leon could not remain hopeful. We quickly returned to our ships. We set sail. Tonight, late, I heard Ponce de Leon talking to the captain. "Imagine what it could have meant," he said. He was looking back to the shoreline. It swept far away from us in the dark of the night. "A fountain of youth. We would live forever. We would have the most important thing in the world. We could stay young forever." The captain shook his head. "Perhaps we are not meant to," he said. Ponce de Leon said nothing more.

Note: Ponce de Leon returned to Florida eight years later. He wanted to claim it as a colony. Again, he looked for the fountain of youth. He did not find it. But in a battle on the Florida coast with Native Americans, many of his men died. He was shot with an arrow that pierced his armor. Ponce de Leon was brought to Cuba, wounded, where he died.

Think About It

1. Why did Ponce de Leon think there was a fountain of youth in Florida?
2. Describe the different ways Ponce de Leon's group was greeted by the Indians.
3. Do you think it would be good to stay young forever? Why or why not?